OXFORD

English
An International Approach

Rachel Redford

OXFORD

UNIVERSITY PRESS

OXFORD
UNIVERSITY PRESS

Great Clarendon Street, Oxford OX2 6DP

Oxford University Press is a department of the University of Oxford.
It furthers the University's objective of excellence in research, scholarship,and
education by publishing worldwide in

Oxford   New York

Auckland Cape Town Dar es Salaam Hong Kong Karachi
Kuala Lumpur Madrid Melbourne Mexico City Nairobi
New Delhi Shanghai Taipei Toronto

With offices in

Argentina Austria Brazil Chile Czech Republic France Greece
Guatemala Hungary Italy Japan Poland Portugal Singapore
South Korea Switzerland Thailand Turkey Ukraine Vietnam

© Oxford University Press

The moral rights of the authors have been asserted

Database right Oxford University Press (maker)

First published 2009

British Library Cataloguing in Publication Data

Data available

ISBN 9780-19-912664-4

30 29 28 27 26

Printed in India by Manipal Technologies Limited

Paper used in the production of this book is a natural, recyclable product made
from wood grown in sustainable forests. The manufacturing process conforms to
the environmental regulations to the country of origin.

Acknowledgements
The Publisher would like to thank the following for permission to reproduce
photographs:
P6 OUP/Photodisc; P8 Nadeem Khawar; P10 Chris Jenner/Shutterstock; P11 Dave
Pape/English Heritage Photo Library; P12 Styve Reineck/Shutterstock; P13 Riccardo
Montanari/Dreamstime.com; P15 Majority World CIC/Photographers Direct; P18
Andrew Holbrooke/Corbis; P20 The London Art Archive/Alamy; P26 Trevor Bauer/
iStockphoto; P28 OUP/Digital Vision; P29 Oleg Kozlov/Shutterstock; P31 Mike
Dunn/NOAA Photo Library; P33 Kapoor Baldev/Sygma/Corbis; P35 A.H.M Rezwan/
AFP; P37ml Anthony Baggett/Dreamstime; P37mr Cliff Fincher/Big Stock Photo;
P37m Paul Banton/Shutterstock; P37bl Geoff Renner/Robert Harding; P37br Ray
roper/Istockphoto; P38 OUP; P39tl Vidler Vidler/Photolibrary; P39tr Greg Gerla/
Photolibrary; P42 OUP/Digital Vision; P45 Landscape with Grey Windy Sky, c.1821-
30 (oil on paper laid down on millboard), Constable, John (1776-1837) / Yale
Center for British Art, Paul Mellon Collection, USA / The Bridgeman Art Library;
P47 Superstock/Photolibrary; P50 Doug Raphael/Shutterstock; P51bl Indiapicture;
P51br Remi Benali/Corbis; P53 Ian Cumming/Getty; P55 Paul Cowan/I-Stock; P58
Roger Rosentreter/I-Stock; P63t Blauel/Gnamm/ARTOTHEK; P63b Wright of Derby,
Joseph (1734-97)/University College of Wales, Aberystwyth, Wales/The Bridgeman
Art Library; P64 Japan Travel Bureau/Photolibrary; P67t Japan Travel Bureau/
Photolibrary; P67b Arko Datta/Reuters; P69 Annett Vauteck/I-Stock; P72 Bridgeman
Art Library; P73 Giuseppe Arcimboldi/Corbis; P74 Rijksmuseum, Amsterdam; P75
Francis G. Mayer/Corbis; P76t Nayef Hashlamoun/Reuters; P76b Laurie Campbell/
NHPA; P78 Chad Ehlers/Alamy; P81t Guentermanaus/Shutterstock; P81m Merten
Merten/Photolibrary; P85 Getty Images; P92 OUP/Photodisc; P93t Pierrette
Guertin/123RF; P93m AGE Fotostock; P95t Zigmund Leszczynski/Photolibrary; P96
Allsorts Media Ltd; P97ml OUP/Digital Vision; P97m OUP/Igor Burchenkov; P97mr
OUP/Digital Vision; P97bl OUP/Amazon-Images; P97b OUP; P97br OUP/Corbis; P98
Zeynep Mufti/Photographers Direct; P101 Dale Robert Franz/Photolibrary; P106
Adisa/Dreamstime.com; P107t Jonathan Olley/Reportage/Getty Images; P107bt Paul
Severn/Getty Images; P107m EA. Janes/Photolibrary; P107b URF URF/Photolibrary;
P107bt Biosphoto/Gunther Michel/Still Pictures; P109bl NASA; P109br Ho New/
Reuters; P110t Map of the Spanish Main (colour litho), Spanish School, (18th
century) / Private Collection / Peter Newark American Pictures / The Bridgeman Art
Library; P110m Canary Islands, from The New Atlas, 1645 (engraving), Dutch School,
(17th century) / Private Collection / Index / The Bridgeman Art Library; P110b
Vladimir Ovchinnikov/I-Stock; P112 OUP/Ingram; P114 Matthew Hertel/I-stock; P115:
I-Stock; P117 Wojtek Kryczka/I-Stock; P121 James Pauls/I-Stock; P136 Jani Bryson/I-
Stock; P137 Jörg Humpe/iStock; P138 Veniamin Kraskov/Fotolia.com; P140 Graeme
Purdy/Istockphoto; P141 The Curtis Collection; P145 Graham Salter/Lebrecht Music
& Arts; P146 Karin Lau/Dreamstime; Thomas M Perkins/Shutterstock; Laurence

Gough/Shutterstock. P151 Wolfgang Kaehler/Alamy; P152 AP Photo/Apichart
Weerawong; P156 Radius Images/Photolibrary; P157 OUP/Stockbyte; P158t Paul
LoveKing/Istockphoto; P158m Jason Lugo/Istockphoto; P158b Rafer/Dreamstime;
P159bl Cenorman/Dreamstime.com; P159b Monkey Business Images/Shutterstock;
P160 123RF; P161 Rhonda Odonnell/Dreamstime.com.

Illustrations on pages 107 and 163 are by Julie Pla.

Cover image: Videowok/iStockphoto

The author and publisher are grateful for permission to reprint the following
copyright material:

Extract from 'Early spring causes havoc for hedgehogs' from *The Evening Standard*,
4.3.2007, reprinted by permission of Solo Syndication for the Evening Standard.

Extract from 'Taj Mahal's walls to receive some TLC', from Wanderlust.co.uk,
21.1.2008, reprinted by permission of Wanderlust.

John Agard, 'I'd Like to Squeeze' from *Get back Pimple* (Viking Childrens' Books, 1996),
copyright © John Agard 1996, reprinted by permission of John Agard c/o Caroline
Sheldon Literary Agency Ltd.

Judy Allen, extract from *Watching* (Walker Books, 2005), coyright © Judy Allen 2005,
reprinted by permission of Walker Books Ltd, London SE11 5HJ.

Shafi Ahmed, 'Bedeh', first published in *The Redbeck Anthology of British South Asian
Poetry* edited by Debjani Chatterjee (Redbeck Press, Bradford, 2000), reprinted by
permission of the author.

Peter Allison, extract from *Whatever You Do Don't Run!* (Nicholas Brealey Publishing,
2007), reprinted by permission of the publisher.

Maya Angelou, lines from 'Human Family', copyright © 1990 Maya Angelou, from *I
Shall Not Be Moved* (Virago, 1990), reprinted by permission of the publishers, Virago,
an imprint of Little, Brown Book Group and Random House, Inc.

Mariya Aziz, 'Alien Abduction', first published in *The Redbeck Anthology of British South
Asian Poetry* edited by Debjani Chatterjee (Redbeck Press, Bradford, 2000): copyright
holder not traced.

Dave Calder, 'Citizen of the World' from *Dolphins Leap Lampposts* (Macmillan, 2002),
reprinted by permission of the author.

Amy Choi, 'The Relative Advantages of Learning My Language', first published in
Growing Up Asian in Australia edited by Alice Pung (Black Inc, 2008), reprinted by
permission of the author.

Jane Clarke, 'Finding a Friend', first published in *I Wanna Be Your Mate* edited by Tony
Bradman (Bloomsbury, 1999), reprinted by permission of the author.

Deborah Ellis, extract from *Mud City* (OUP, 2003), copyright © Deborah Ellis 2003,
reprinted by permission of Oxford University Press.

Jackie Kay, 'Bush Fire' from *Red Cherry Red* (Bloomsbury, 2007), reprinted by
permission of Bloomsbury Publishing Plc.

Elizabeth Laird, extract from *Red Sky in the Morning* (Macmillan Children's Books,
2001), reprinted by permission of the publishers.

Michael Morpurgo, extract from *Dear Olly* (Collins, 2000), copyright © Michael
Morpurgo 2000, and extract from *Toro! Toro!* (Collins, 2001), copyright © Michael
Morpurgo 2001, reprinted by permission of HarperCollins Publishers Ltd.

Lupenga Mphande, 'Why the Old Woman Limps' from *The Heinemann Book of African
Poetry in English* edited by Adewale Maja-Pearce (Heinemann, 1990), reprinted by
permission of Pearson Education Ltd.

Naomi Shihab Nye, extract from the poet's introduction to *19 Varieties of Gazelle: Poems
of the Middle East* (Greenwillow Books, 1994), copyright © Naomi Shihab Nye 2002,
reprinted by permission of HarperCollins Publishers, USA.

Scott O'Dell, extract from *Sing Down the Moon* (Bantam Doubleday Dell, 1970),
copyright © 1970 by Scott O'Dell, renewed 1998 by Elizabeth Hall, reprinted by
permission of Houghton Mifflin Harcourt Publishing Company and McIntosh & Otis,
Inc. All rights reserved.

Linda Sue Park: extract from *A Single Shard* (OUP, 2001), copyright © Linda Sue Park
2001, reprinted by permission of Oxford University Press.

Bill Paterson, extract from *Tales from the Back Green* (Hodder & Stoughton, 2008),
copyright © Bill Paterson 2008, reprinted by permission of the publishers and David
Godwin Associates Ltd

Suzanne Fisher Staples, adapted extract from *Shabanu: Daughter of the Wind* (Walker
Books, 2002), text copyright © Suzanne Fisher Staples 1989, reprinted by permission
of the publishers, Walker Books Ltd, London SE11 5HJ and Alfred A Knopf, an
imprint of Random House Children's Books, a division of Random House, Inc.

Laura Ingalls Wilder: extract from *Little House on the Prairie* (Egmont, 2000), copyright
Laura Ingalls Wilder 1953, © renewed 1963 by Roger L MacBride, reprinted by
permission of the publishers.

Although we have made every effort to trace and contact all copyright holders
before publication this has not been possible in all cases. If notified, the publisher
will rectify any errors or omissions at the earliest opportunity.

Contents

Oxford English: An International Approach, Student Book 1

Oxford English: An International Approach, Student Book 1 is the first in a series of four books designed for students. The series is aimed at those with English as a first language or a strong second language who are taking English as a subject. The books provide students with a wonderful selection of fiction and non-fiction extracts from across the globe and are grouped into themes such as 'Water', 'Catastrophes' and 'Feeding the world'.

The unique variety of textual material provides a backdrop against which students can improve their skills in reading, writing, speaking and listening. The ethical concepts and ideas will engage students in topics of real concern to them. Many extracts and activities relate to everyday life and pursuits such as art, travel, adventure and technology. This unique mix of content will enable students to learn about their own identity and their place in the world, and to explore the ways in which their personal lives are connected to the global picture. The extracts, and the accompanying activities and questions, will encourage students to make these important connections, and to think critically.

A strong focus is placed on writing activities. Often a writing assignment will come out of a reading activity so that students have a model on which to base their own writing. The writing activities have been designed to motivate students to write, and to expose them to different types of texts.

The international approach is an important aim of the series. From the many unusual and exciting extracts – which come from all over the world, from Afghanistan to Australia, from Zanzibar to Japan, from the Middle East to Mexico – students will increase their understanding and appreciation of the world. Attractive maps place the texts in their global contexts. The following useful features support vocabulary development and group discussions:

Wordpool Acquiring vocabulary is an essential part of any learning for both first and second language students. The wordpool features the words which students will need to understand each text. An emphasis is placed on encouraging students to identify for themselves the words they need to know. For class discussion, teachers can place large wordpools on the blackboard and direct a class activity to identify unknown words from any reading or listening activity.

Glossary The many glossaries explain technical vocabulary and significant words of cultural relevance. Through this, students will improve their vocabulary and develop an understanding of other cultures.

Word origins Basic etymology and word origins are discussed in this vocabulary feature. Students will begin to understand the development of language and appreciate how languages share vocabulary.

Talking points Students will be encouraged to talk with a partner or to discuss in groups. Speaking is an important skill in language learning, encouraging students to express opinions, and develop a greater appreciation and understanding of a topic, while improving their language skills.

Toolkit Students' attention will be drawn to important language and grammar concepts. Exercises to practise these skills are provided in the workbook.

Comprehension Questions are provided to increase students' understanding and comprehension of the texts. These questions develop in complexity for a deeper understanding and appreciation of the text.

Looking closely These questions require students to look back through the text and re-read and investigate aspects of language usage or vocabulary. These questions range from using context clues to define meanings, to identifying metaphors and similes.

Journals Throughout these units there are suggested topics for students to write about. Students should write about any aspect of the topic from a personal point of view. They should not be graded on the writing – it is a chance for students to write as a direct form of expression in a separate journal or notebook. Journals can be used to link lessons by asking students to share what they have written with the class, perhaps at the start of a lesson.

The Teacher's Guide This companion publication provides ideas for introducing topics and extending lessons, rubrics for writing activities and all the answers to the exercises in the student book and the workbook. In addition there is an audio CD of readings from extracts in the student book, as indicated by the CD symbol. 💿

The Workbook An 80-page workbook provides extra practice exercises for vocabulary and grammar along with additional support for the writing assignments. 🆆

And, finally, to acknowledgements. This publication is dedicated to all the students who use this book. It would not have been possible without the permission of the authors and artists who have kindly granted us the rights to reproduce excerpts and illustrations of their work. Special thanks to academic advisor Patricia Mertin, series editor Carolyn Lee, production editor Eve Sullivan and Mara Singer for the design concept, who have all worked with such enthusiasm on the development of the material for publication.

RACHEL REDFORD, 2009

Water, water

How do we use water?

In this unit you will:

Experience
- Pakistan
- the Isle of Wight
- Syria
- Bangladesh

Read
- prose fiction
- travel writing
- a postcard
- a poem

Create
- a composition
- a leaflet
- an account

Water, water, everywhere,
Nor any drop to drink.

From 'The Rime of the Ancient Mariner' by Samuel Taylor Coleridge, 1798

What is the situation described in the quotation above? There is a clue in the title of the poem: a 'mariner' is a sailor.

In Coleridge's poem the sailors, surrounded by salty seawater, are desperate for water to drink. It is impossible for anyone to survive for long without fresh water.

Talking points

1 How is water important to you?
2 How much of a role does water play in your daily routines?

Prose fiction

From *Shabanu: Daughter of the Wind* by Suzanne Fisher Staples

In the following text, a twelve-year-old girl, Shabanu, describes her morning ritual. She lives with her family and their camels in the Cholistan Desert in Pakistan. Water is extremely precious to them. When their water source dries up, they move on to another part of the desert.

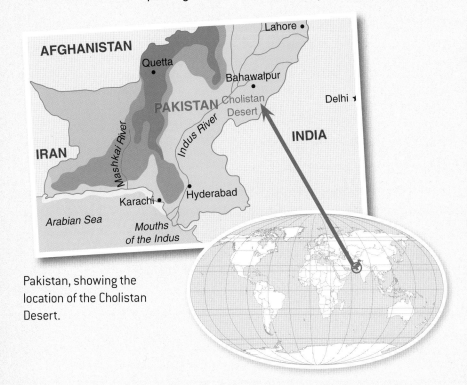

Pakistan, showing the location of the Cholistan Desert.

Word origins

Some of the Urdu names in this novel are similar to English names. *Shabanu* is named after the eighth Islamic month, Shaban. In English the girl's names April, May and June are all the names of months. *Phulan*, the name of Shabanu's older sister, means 'flower'. In English the girls' names Rose, Daisy and Heather are all flower names. *Mithoo* is an affectionate name meaning 'sweet'. In English, little children are sometimes called 'sweetie'.

ᗦ **Morning in the Desert** ᗧ

The sky is pearl-grey when I awake. My sister Phulan pushes me out of bed. Yawning and rubbing my eyes, I tie a piece of soap into the corner of my chador. I pick up two earthen pots and a padded ring to balance one pot on my head. The
5 other fits under my arm, balanced on my hip. My camel, Mithoo, and I set off for the water hole, the toba. Mithoo's small brass bell jingles cheerfully as he moves his head, impatient for me to fold back the reed door which leads from our courtyard to the outside. I make Mithoo carry the empty
10 goatskin to the toba.

At the toba I look out over our dwindling water supply. We probably have a month, perhaps three weeks, before the

GLOSSARY

Cholistan comes from the Urdu word *cholna* meaning to move or walk, and *-stan* meaning land or place of. You will see why when you read the story.

Chador is an Urdu (originally Persian) word for the shawl or veil worn by Muslim women and girls to cover their heads and shoulders.

A **toba** is a water hole.

water disappears. The monsoon will not begin for another two months. Then will be the time for flowers, mushrooms,
15 weddings and water, but not now. Two-toed camel footprints are baked into the shiny clay at the outer edges of the toba. I lift my skirt with one hand, and the mud squirts between my toes as I enter the water. I push aside the green scum that floats just under the surface and place the edge of my chador
20 over the mouth of the water pot to filter out impurities. I take the filled pot to the bathing rock at the edge of the toba and lift my tunic over my head. I throw my hair forward and pour water over it.

The sun edges over the horizon. I can feel its heat on my
25 back and shoulders as the water trickles over my scalp. I rub the soap into my hair. I squeeze my eyes shut, letting the soapy water drain down my shoulders and neck, rubbing into my skin before rinsing off to preserve every drop. Mama used to bath my sister and me with a single cup of water
30 when we were small.

The sun is extremely hot as I walk back. Over the next week we watch our water dwindle yet further. In the heat of the afternoons, before the daily wind and dust arrive, we dry herbs. As the precious water slips away with the hot desert
35 wind, we also make our preparations for leaving the toba and moving on.

SUZANNE FISHER STAPLES

Women carrying water jars in the Cholistan Desert.

8

Comprehension

1 What does Shabanu take with her to the water hole?

2 How does Shabanu manage to carry two pots to the water hole?

3 What changes will the monsoon bring to the family's way of life?

4 How does Shabanu make sure that the water she collects in her pot is clean?

5 Why do you think the water level is so low?

Looking closely

1 How does Shabanu describe the morning sky? (line 1)

2 'Goatskin' is made from two words put together. What do you suppose a goatskin is? What is it used for? (line 10)

3 Find a word that means 'getting smaller'. (paragraph 4)

4 What word is used to emphasize how hot the sun is? (paragraph 4)

Toolkit

W Notice that this story is written in the *present tense*. To change it to the *past tense,* use the simple past tense form of the verb.

Present tense: I make Mithoo carry the empty goatskin.

Past tense: I made Mithoo carry the empty goatskin.

Writing a composition

In the story *Morning in the Desert,* water is a luxury for Shabanu and her family and they use as little as possible. When they were young, her mother washed the children in just one cupful! You wash every morning too, but you probably don't have to walk to a water hole with a camel. How is your day similar to Shabanu's day? How is it different?

- W Create a Venn diagram that compares Shabanu's way of life to your own. You have probably used Venn diagrams in mathematics, but you can also use them to arrange ideas.
- Write a three-paragraph composition in which you compare Shabanu's life with your own. The Venn diagram will help you to decide what to put in each paragraph.

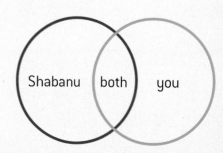

How did people get water in the past?

From the earliest times of civilization, people have faced the problem of getting water up from under the ground.

In Britain there are a lot of old castles and fortifications. Long ago, people lived inside these walls so a source of water was essential. Today, the castles are attractive places for visitors.

Carisbrooke Castle was built in the Middle Ages on the Isle of Wight, an island off the south coast of Britain. The following leaflet is about the donkey-powered well there.

Carisbrooke Castle, Isle of Wight
Have a great day out and learn about the island's history!

The gatehouse entrance to Carisbrooke Castle.

Carisbrooke Castle can be found right in the middle of the Isle of Wight. The main castle walls that stand today were built by Norman rulers in the 11th and 12th centuries.

The hill the castle is on was used as a site for several previous strongholds. A hill is a great place to build a castle because it can be defended from enemy attack.

But just as important for the people living in a castle is access to water! At Carisbrooke Castle you can still see the unique way that water was brought into the castle.

Come and see the only donkey-powered well in Britain!

- ❖ The well at Carisbrooke Castle was dug in 1136 when the original water source dried up.
- ❖ A wooden bucket was used to collect water from the well, which is 49 metres deep.
- ❖ A well-house and treadwheel were built in 1291 and donkey power was introduced to the castle.
- ❖ In 1587 the treadwheel was rebuilt by later island rulers. You can see one of the six castle donkeys working the treadwheel today!

Water being drawn from the well, just as it was many centuries ago.

Talking points

1 Does the leaflet make you think you would like to go there? Why? Or why not?

2 How effective are the different types of sentences used in the leaflet?

3 Can you think of any ways in which the leaflet could be improved?

Toolkit

The passive voice is useful when you want to describe how something was done to someone or something, without saying who did it.

Example: Carisbrooke Castle was built in the Middle Ages.

The *passive voice* is formed by using the appropriate form of the verb *to be* plus the past participle. It can also be formed using modal verbs.

Making a leaflet

 Use the information below about the water wheels at Hama to plan and design a leaflet about them. Do some additional research.

- Draft your own ideas for a leaflet to encourage people to come and see the amazing water wheels.
- When you have finished, compare your leaflet plan with those of others in your group. Which features are most successful?
- Look at other leaflets on places of interest near you. Once you have a good idea of how leaflets can be designed, produce a final colourful version.

> **GLOSSARY**
>
> An **aqueduct** is an artificial channel for carrying water. An aqueduct can be below or above ground. Above-ground aqueducts also bridge gaps.
>
> To **irrigate** means to bring water through artifical channels to supplement rainfall and support more intensive farming practices.

The water wheels (*norias*) of Hama, Syria

- Hama is about 40 kilometres from Aleppo in Syria.
- Settlements in Hama go back to the Bronze Age and the Iron Age.
- Hama's water wheels (*norias*) are up to 20 metres in diameter, the height of a five-storey building.
- *Norias* have been in Hama since at least the fifth century.
- 17 of the 30 *norias* built in the 13th century still survive today.
- The wheels bring up water from the River Orontes, as it is lower than the land.
- *Norias* are driven by the current of the water acting upon the paddles, and require no other form of power to keep them going.
- Water fills and drives the wooden boxes that empty into aqueducts at the top of the wheel's rotation.

- Wheels were used to supply the town with water and for irrigating crops in the surrounding farmland.
- Although no longer applied to practical use, the wheels still turn in spring and summer for the benefit of tourists.
- Creaking and groaning as they bring up the water, they are a wonderful sight and a reminder of Syria's fascinating past.

Hama, Syria

SYRIAN ARAB REPUBLIC

Dear Jelle,

We had a wonderful time in Hama, where they have these amazing old water wheels (norias) from the 13th century. They scoop the water up from the river in boxes to supply whole towns with water, and also the local farmlands (after being channelled through aqueducts). Or, at least they used to. These days, it's just for the tourists, but the wheels are magnificent to see in action, creaking and groaning like big old ghost ships! Wish you were here, seeing it all with us.

Love Karina xxx

Jelle Martinsen
1e Kanaalsbrug
Leeuwarden
8933
THE NETHERLANDS

Journal

Describe something you learned while on holiday.

Who lives on water?

When you were discussing ways you use water, did anyone think of using water as a place to live?

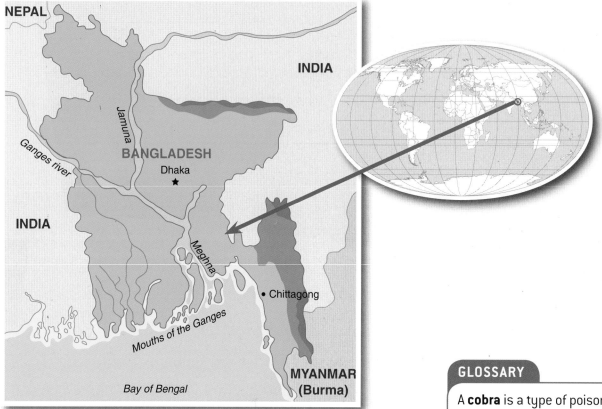

Map of Bangladesh, showing its big river system.

Prose non-fiction

From *Going to Extremes* by Nick Middleton

The following story is about the river gypsies who live and work on their boats in Bangladesh. Look at the map to see just how large the river delta is in Bangladesh.

The river gypsies of Bangladesh are renowned for their skills in handling snakes. The writer met the river gypsies on his travels and the following text recalls an occasion when these skills were put to good use.

Word origins

Gypsies were originally thought to have come from Egypt, which is where the name comes from. Gypsies are travelling people and their language, Romany, is related to Hindi. Today there are gypsies all over the world.

GLOSSARY

A **cobra** is a type of poisonous snake found in Asia and Africa.

A **delta** is land formed at the mouth of a river by the mud and sand brought there by the water.

Wordpool

to dangle (line 7)

commotion (10)

to coax (12)

sideboard (23)

proceeding (26)

expertly (30)

to cower (34)

faithful (36)

ʅ **The River Gypsies** ʆ

My Indian friend, Babu, and I stood amongst the crowd watching the river gypsies with their snakes. Beside them were several wooden boxes in which they kept their snakes. From one of these boxes one of the gypsies had produced half a dozen small

5   snakes which were winding themselves round his wrists like bright green bangles. The other gypsy, who wore a purple headscarf tied round his forehead, was dangling his hands in front of a hooded cobra which was rising up from another box. The crowd watched in horror and delight.

10   Suddenly there was a small commotion in the crowd and an old man came forward and spoke to the river gypsies, who immediately began to coax their snakes back into their boxes.

'The old man has a snake in his house,' Babu explained to me.

A river gypsy with his hooded cobras, Bangladesh.

15　The crowd followed the river gypsies to the old man's house, the backyard of which sloped down to the flooded fields. One of the river men gathered some earth from the entrance and rubbed it between his hands. He smelt it and gave it to his colleague in the purple headscarf to do the same.

20　'If the earth smells of fish, then the men know there's a snake inside,' Babu whispered to me.

The river gypsies entered the main room which had a bed on one side, and a neat row of cooking pots hung above a sideboard on the other. The owner of the house, evidently pleased to see

25　a foreigner, beckoned me into his bedroom and pointed to the bed. This was the safest place from which to watch the proceedings. Suddenly there was a commotion beneath the sideboard and the river gypsy with the purple headscarf darted underneath it. He emerged holding a full-sized cobra as long as his arm. The

30　snake hissed as the river gypsy expertly twisted his arm to prevent the snake from striking him. The crowd let out a collective gasp as he began to force the cobra into one of his boxes.

But the show was not over yet. The other river gypsy had his head beneath the bed on which I was cowering. He emerged in

35　a flash holding a second cobra, just as long as the first.

'Husband and wife!' cried Babu. 'Cobras are faithful partners. They always travel together!'

Nick Middleton

Comprehension

1　What caused the small commotion in the crowd?

2　Why did the gypsies immediately start to put their snakes back in their boxes?

3　How did the river gypsies know that there was a snake inside the house?

4　How did the old man show his pleasure at seeing a foreigner in his house?

5　Why didn't the snake from underneath the sideboard bite the man?

Looking closely

1   How does the writer describe the way the snakes were winding around the gypsy's wrists? (lines 5 and 6)

2   Why has the writer used the words 'horror and delight' to describe the way the crowd was feeling? (line 9)

3   What word for a disturbance is used twice?

4   What were the people in the crowd thinking when they 'let out a collective gasp'? (line 31)

5   Why is what Babu says about the cobras being 'husband and wife' funny? (line 36)

Toolkit

Writing *direct speech* usually involves putting quotation marks around the words that are said. *Indirect speech* usually involves changing the sentence to the past tense, adding the word 'that' and changing the pronoun.

Example: 'My friend needs the snake catchers,' Babu said to me.
          Babu told me that his friend needed the snake catchers.

Writing an account

The River Gypsies is written in the first person, which is the writer's point of view. The 'I' is the writer himself, and he is retelling the events as he remembers them. He often uses the simple past tense to describe what happened. The text presents things in a chronological order. (That means that things are told in the order in which they happen.)

Now pretend that you are the old man who had the snakes taken from his home. You meet a neighbour who was away when the river gypsies came, and she asks you to explain what happened.

● Write an account from the old man's perspective. Make it sound very exciting.
● Remember to write in the first person and mainly use the past tense – but watch out for any irregular verbs.

You will need to make use of the details from the text, including what Babu says.

Poem

The following poem was written by Shafi Ahmed, who was born in Bangladesh in 1937. The first-person 'I' in this poem is a river gypsy in Bangladesh. Bedeh is a name for the river gypsies.

Poetry often creates images in your head. After you have read or listened to the poem, choose some lines from 'Bedeh'. Illustrate the lines you have chosen using pictures and sketches. You may choose to make the words part of your illustration.

ഔ Bedeh ര

This is the name of my clan.
I am a water-gypsy
on the turbulent rivers of Bangladesh.
My boat is home
5　to me, my wife, and our children.

I have some knowledge of words
and wild herbs.
I treat snake-bites, drive out evil spirits,
and attempt things which others dare not.
10　Tigers, robbers, snakes, demons, storms
all seem to leave me alone!

Wordpool

clan (line 1)

turbulent (3)

to attempt (9)

anchorage (19)

to marvel (27)

My needs are small and simple.
They are easily met
from day to day, from hand to mouth,
15 from one river settlement
to the next.

Sometimes in fine weather
I row out to the river's end.
I meet many ships at the anchorage.
20 The crew exchanges foodstuffs,
old clothes, newspapers,
empty cans and bottles
with my beads, bangles,
bamboo-toys and seashells.

25 Once I had a chance to board
an English ship.
I marvelled at the ocean-going craft.
But the Captain, he marvelled: at me,
at the size of my boat,
30 at how we had survived, at how we live!
He wrote down our names,
and other things in his notebook.
He said, one day he would write about us.

I cannot imagine
35 Why anyone would want
To do that!

SHAFI AHMED

Comprehension

1 Apart from treating snake-bites, what does the river gypsy do?

2 What does the river gypsy do in fine weather?

3 What is it about the river gypsy that causes the Captain to marvel at him?

4 What does the Captain do with his notebook?

5 What gives the reader the impression that the river gypsy has a humble opinion of himself?

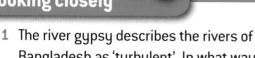

Looking closely

1 The river gypsy describes the rivers of Bangladesh as 'turbulent'. In what ways would turbulent rivers make life difficult for the river gypsy? (line 3)

2 What is another word for 'demon' used in the poem? (line 8)

3 Why do you think tigers, robbers, snakes, demons and storms could be dangerous for the river gypsy? (line 10)

4 The gypsy lives a 'hand-to-mouth' existence. What does this expression mean? (line 14)

Thinking about water

When you were brainstorming the ways in which we use water, did you think about going to the beach?

Look at this painting by the French artist Edgar Degas, painted in the nineteenth century. Degas liked to paint ordinary people at leisure. At this time in France it was becoming fashionable to visit the seaside. In this image a woman combs the hair of the young girl, who has fallen asleep in the sun.

Beach Scene by Edgar Degas, painted in 1868–77.

Looking closely

1 What is happening in the painting?

2 How would you describe the mood of the painting?

3 How do we know that the young girl has been swimming?

4 How does Degas create the effect of bright sunlight?

Journal

Imagine you are one of the characters in the painting and write a journal entry about your day.

Extension reading

From *Little House on the Prairie* by Laura Ingalls Wilder

This is the story of a family of settlers who travelled to the western part of America before it was part of the United States. Many families joined 'wagon trains' in search of wealth, excitement and a better life. Here the father of the family finds trouble while digging a well.

Wordpool

stout (line 19)

scaly (21)

blistering (28)

fierce (31)

to unravel (130)

GLOSSARY

A **windlass** is a tool for lifting heavy weights.

Plumb tuckered out is a phrase that means 'completely exhausted'.

Quicksand is sand that is unstable and dangerous.

A **tow sack** is a cloth sack.

A **patchwork quilt** is a blanket or bed cover, made of patches of material

Pa means 'Father'.

Ma means 'Mother'.

 ✄ **Fresh Water to Drink** ✄

Next morning he marked a large circle in the grass near the corner of the house. With his spade he cut the sod inside the circle, and lifted it up in large pieces. Then he began to shovel out the earth, digging himself deeper and deeper down.

5   Mary and Laura must not go near the well while Pa was digging. Even when they couldn't see his head any more, shovelfuls of earth came flying up. At last the spade flew up and fell in the grass. Then Pa jumped. His hands caught hold of the sod, then one elbow gripped it, and then the other elbow, and with a heave

10 Pa came rolling out. 'I can't throw the dirt out from any deeper,' he said.

He had to have help now. So he took his gun and rode away on Patty. When he came back he brought a plump rabbit, and he had traded work with Mr Scott. Mr Scott would help

15 him dig this well, and then he would help dig Mr Scott's well.

Ma and Laura and Mary had not seen Mr and Mrs Scott. Their house was hidden somewhere in a little valley on the prairie.

Laura had seen the smoke rising up from it, and that was all. At dawn next morning Mr Scott came. He was short and stout.

20 His hair was bleached by the sun and his skin was bright red and scaly. He did not tan; he peeled.

'It's this blasted sun and wind,' he said. 'Beg your pardon, ma'am, but it's enough to make a saint use strong language. I might as well be a snake, the way I keep on shedding my skin

25 in this country.'

Laura liked him. Every morning, as soon as the dishes were washed and the beds made, she ran out to watch Mr Scott and Pa working at the well. The sunshine was blistering, even the winds were hot, and the prairie grasses were turning yellow.

30 Mary preferred to stay in the house and sew on her patchwork quilt. But Laura liked the fierce light and the sun and the wind, and she couldn't stay away from the well. But she was not allowed to go near its edge.

Pa and Mr Scott had made a stout windlass. It stood over the

35 well, and two buckets hung from it on the ends of a rope. When the windlass was turned, one bucket went down into the well and the other bucket came up. In the morning, Mr Scott slid down the rope and dug. He filled the bucket with earth, almost as fast as Pa could haul them up and empty them. After dinner,

40 Pa slid down the rope into the well, and Mr Scott hauled up the buckets.

Every morning, before Pa would let Mr Scott go down the rope, he set a candle in a bucket and lighted it and lowered it to the bottom. Once Laura peeped over the edge and she saw the candle

45 brightly burning, far down in the dark hole in the ground.

Then Pa would say, 'Seems to be all right,' and he would pull up the bucket and blow out the candle.

'That's all foolishness, Ingalls,' Mr Scott said. 'The well was all right yesterday.'

50 'You can't ever tell,' Pa replied. 'Better safe than sorry.'

Laura did not know what danger Pa was looking for by that candle-light. She did not ask, because Pa and Mr Scott were busy. She meant to ask later, but she forgot.

55 One morning Mr Scott came while Pa was eating breakfast. They heard him shout: 'Hi, Ingalls! It's sun-up. Let's go!' Pa drank his coffee and went out.

The windlass began to creak and Pa began to whistle. Laura and Mary were washing the dishes and Ma was making the big bed, when Pa's whistling stopped. They heard him say, 'Scott!'
60 He shouted, 'Scott! Scott!' Then he called: 'Caroline! Come quick!'

Ma ran out of the house. Laura ran after her.

'Scott's fainted, or something, down there,' Pa said. 'I've got to go down after him.'

65 'Did you send down the candle?' Ma asked.

'No. I thought he had. I asked him if it was all right, and he said it was.' Pa cut the empty bucket off the rope and tied the rope firmly to the windlass.

'Charles, you can't. You mustn't,' Ma said.

70 'Caroline, I've got to.'

'You can't. Oh, Charles, no!'

'I'll make it all right. I won't breathe till I get out. We can't let him die down there.'

75 Ma said, fiercely: 'Laura, keep back!' So Laura kept back. She stood against the house and shivered.

'No, no, Charles! I can't let you,' Ma said. 'Get on Patty and go for help.'

'There isn't time.'

80 'Charles, if I can't pull you up – if you keel over down there and I can't pull you up –'

'Caroline, I've got to,' Pa said. He swung into the well. His head slid out of sight, down the rope.

Ma crouched and shaded her eyes, staring down into the well.

85 All over the prairie meadowlarks were rising, singing, flying straight up into the sky. The wind was blowing warmer, but Laura was cold.

Suddenly Ma jumped up and seized the handle of the windlass. She tugged at it with all her might. The rope strained and the

90 windlass creaked. Laura thought that Pa had keeled over, down in the dark bottom of the well, and Ma couldn't pull him up. But the windlass turned a little, and then a little more.

Pa's hand came up, holding to the rope. His other hand reached above it and took hold of the rope. Then Pa's head came up.

95 His arm held on to the windlass. Then somehow he got to the ground and sat there.

The windlass whirled round and there was a thud deep down in the well. Pa struggled to get up and Ma said: 'Sit still, Charles! Laura, get some water. Quick!'

100 Laura ran. She came hurrying back, lugging the pail of water. Pa and Ma were both turning the windlass. The rope slowly wound itself up, and the bucket came up out of the well, and tied to the bucket and the rope was Mr Scott. His arms and legs and his head hung and wobbled, his mouth was partly open and

105 his eyes half shut.

Pa tugged him on to the grass. Pa rolled him over and he flopped where he was rolled. Pa felt his wrist and listened at his chest, and then Pa lay down beside him.

'He's breathing,' Pa said. 'He'll be all right, in the air. I'm all

110 right, Caroline. I'm plumb tuckered out, that's all.'

'Well!' Ma scolded. 'I should think you would be. Of all the senseless performances! My goodness gracious! Scaring a body to death, all for want of a little reasonable care! My goodness I –' She covered her face with her apron and burst out crying.

115 That was a terrible day.

'I don't want a well,' Ma sobbed. 'It isn't worth it. I won't have you running such risks!'

Mr Scott had breathed a kind of gas that stays deep in the ground. It stays at the bottom of wells because it is heavier than
120 the air. It cannot be seen or smelled, but no one can breathe it very long and live. Pa had gone down into that gas to tie Mr Scott to the rope so that he could be pulled up out of the gas.

When Mr Scott was able, he went home. Before he went he said to Pa: 'You were right about that candle business, Ingalls. I
125 thought it was all foolishness and I would not bother with it, but I've found out my mistake.'

'Well,' said Pa, 'where a light can't live, I know I can't. And I like to be safe when I can be. But all's well that ends well.'

Pa rested awhile. He had breathed a little of the gas and he felt
130 like resting. But that afternoon he unravelled a thread from a tow sack, and he took a little powder from his powder-horn. He tied the powder in a piece of cloth with one end of the tow string in the powder.

'Come along, Laura,' he said, 'and I'll show you something.'

135 They went to the well. Pa lighted the end of the string and waited until the spark was crawling quickly along it. Then he dropped the little bundle into the well.

In a minute they heard a muffled bang! and a puff of smoke came out of the well. 'That will bring the gas,' Pa said.

140 When the smoke was all gone, he let Laura light the candle and stand beside him while he let it down. All the way down in the dark hole the little candle kept on burning like a star.

So next day Pa and Mr Scott went on digging the well. But they always sent the candle down every morning.

145 There began to be a little water in the well, but it was not enough. The buckets came up full of mud, and Pa and Mr Scott worked every day in deeper mud. In the mornings when the candle went down, it lighted oozing-wet walls, and candlelight sparkled in rings over the water when the bucket
150 struck bottom.

Pa stood knee deep in water and bailed out bucketfuls before he could begin digging in the mud.

One day when he was digging, a loud shout came echoing up. Ma ran out of the house and Laura ran to the well. 'Pull,
155 Scott! Pull!' Pa yelled. A swishing, gurgling sound echoed down there. Mr Scott turned the windlass as fast as he could, and Pa came up climbing hand over hand up the rope.

160 'I'm blamed if that's not quicksand!' Pa gasped, as he stepped on to the ground, muddy and dripping. 'I was pushing down hard on the spade, when all of a sudden it went down, the whole length of the handle. And water came pouring all up around me.'

165 'A good six feet of this rope's wet,' Mr Scott said, winding it up. The bucket was full of water. 'You showed sense in getting out of that hand over hand, Ingalls. That water came up faster than I could pull you out.' Then Mr Scott slapped his thigh and shouted, 'I'm blasted if you didn't bring up the spade!'

Sure enough, Pa had saved his spade.

170 In a little while the well was almost full of water. A circle of blue sky lay not far down in the ground, and when Laura looked at it, a little girl's head looked up at her. When she waved her hand, a hand on the water's surface waved, too.

175 The water was clear and cold and good. Laura thought she had never tasted anything so good as those long, cold drinks of water. Pa hauled no more stale, warm water from the creek. He built a solid platform over the well, and a heavy cover for the hole that let the water-bucket through. Laura must never touch that cover. But whenever she or Mary was
180 thirsty, Ma lifted the cover and drew a dripping bucket of cold, fresh water from that well.

LAURA INGALLS WILDER

Comprehension

1 Why does Pa need help digging his well?
2 What danger is Pa looking for by sending his candle into the well?
3 Why doesn't Ma want Pa to go into the well after Mr Scott?
4 How is Mr Scott saved?

Talking point

Have you or someone you know ever had to do something dangerous?

Climate

How are animals affected by changes in climate?

In this unit you will:

Experience
- Canada and the Arctic
- Bangladesh
- Australia
- South Africa

Read
- a news article
- a composition
- poetry
- a weather report

Create
- a newspaper report
- a poem
- a weather forecast

Scientists fear global warming could drive polar bears to extinction some time this century.

National Geographic, June 2007

Talking points

1 What do you know about climate change?

2 How might the situation of the polar bears be connected with climate change?

3 Discuss other recent news stories about the effects of climate change.

News article

The news article on the next page is about hedgehogs, which are now an endangered species in Britain. A journalist explains how hedgehogs have been affected by unusual weather conditions.

Wordpool

havoc	spines
disorientated	dehydrated
founder	Make your own
to forage	wordpool of any other
distressed	unfamiliar words you
	come across.

Word Origins

Hibernation is the resting or sleeping state in which some animals pass the winter. This word derives from the Latin word for 'winter'.

The word *nocturnal* also comes from Latin, from the word for 'night'. A nocturnal animal is more active at night than in the daytime.

Early Spring Causes Havoc for Hedgehogs

They should be curled up, enjoying a four-month winter sleep. But the warm British winter has tricked thousands of young hedgehogs into thinking that spring is well under way.

Once awake, they are unable to find enough food because their usual diet of snails and insects do not start appearing until later in the year. Weakened and disorientated, many hedgehogs do not survive unless they are found by members of the public and taken to an animal hospital.

Hedgehogs are usually fast asleep through the winter.

Staff at a wildlife hospital near Aylesbury, Buckinghamshire, have reported a surge in the number of the creatures brought in. About 550 hedgehogs have been handed in, compared with 300 over the same period last winter.

Hedgehogs normally hibernate between late December and the middle of April. But many are tricked into coming out of hibernation early by the warm weather, only to be caught out by cold snaps or the lack of food. Traditionally, the creatures are nocturnal, but increasing numbers are being spotted during the daytime in the desperate hunt for food.

'We have got hedgehogs everywhere,' said the hospital founder, Les Stocker. 'There's nothing for them to eat outside and when they come in they are in real trouble. They will stay with us throughout the winter while we fatten them up before releasing them back into the wild in April when they will

have enough energy to forage for food by themselves. It is usually the young hedgehogs which get into trouble because they often don't have enough fat reserves to survive.'

Hedgehogs are not the only animals to be affected by the unusual weather conditions. Newts, bats and grass snakes, which should all be in hibernation, have been found in distress by members of the public and taken to the rescue hospital. Butterflies and bumblebees that do not usually emerge until spring have been spotted as early as December.

'This change in temperature is a big problem,' said Nick Collison, head of conservation policy at the Woodland Trust. 'Our winters are becoming more topsy-turvy with a particular feature now being very mild periods followed by sudden cold snaps,' he said.
THE DAILY MAIL, 4 March 2007

Almost all scientists believe that the way human beings live is having an effect on the Earth's climate. Many different consequences have been suggested, including the loss of particular species of animals and plants, and changes in weather patterns.

Writing a newspaper article

Read the fact file about polar bears on page 31. Then use some of the information to create a news story of your own. Use the article about hedgehogs as a model, and begin with a catchy phrase or question. Notice how the writer of the article on hedgehogs has tried to answer certain questions for the reader, such as:

- What is the problem?
- What has caused the problem?
- What evidence is there, and what have experts said?
- What is being done about the problem?

Use these questions and the fact file to write your own newspaper article about how polar bears are affected by climate change.

FACT FILE

- The Arctic's climate is changing and global warming is affecting polar bears.

- The Arctic is experiencing the warmest air temperatures for four centuries.

- Scientists believe Arctic sea ice has decreased by 14% since the 1970s.

- The Polar Bears International website (www.polarbearsinternational.org) states that there are between 20,000 and 25,000 polar bears worldwide. Of these, 60% are in Canada.

- The website explains that the melting ice reduces the areas in which polar bears can hunt for food.

- Canada's western Hudson Bay polar bear population has dropped by 22% since 1987, according to a study by the US Geological Survey and Canadian Wildlife Service.

- Henry Kacprzyk, a Philadelphia zoo curator, has handouts and leaflets ready for visitors to explain how reducing energy use and recycling can cut the greenhouse gas pollution that contributes to global warming.

- Rosa Meehan, who heads the marine mammal programme for the US Fish and Wildlife Service in Alaska, says that cutting greenhouse gas pollution now and in the future will improve the polar bears' long-term outlook.

1 How many polar bears are there in Canada?

2 What danger to polar bears is caused by melting snow?

Analysing the data

Make sure you understand the significance of the information presented in the fact file on page 31. This will help you with your newspaper article.

Draw a pie chart to show the percentage of sea ice that has disappeared in the past 35 years.

How many polar bears from every 1,000 have disappeared from western Hudson Bay in Canada since 1987?

Undertake further research to identify further habitats for polar bears. Where else on the map below do polar bears roam?

Map of the Arctic, showing the location of Hudson Bay and the North Pole.

How is climate change affecting the way people live?

Look back at the map on page 14 showing Bangladesh and its river delta. Can you see why the country suffers from frequent floods? Bangladesh is one of the countries in the world most vulnerable to the effects of global warming. Floods have worsened the outlook for the 150 million inhabitants, most of whom are desperately poor. Glaciers in the Himalayas have melted more than in the past, and scientists say that Bangladesh may lose as much as 20 per cent of its land to flooding by 2030. Twenty million people unable to farm their flooded land could then become 'climate refugees'.

Wordpool

vulnerable	refugees
inhabitants	bleak
desperately	

GLOSSARY

A **glacier** is a huge mass of ice slowing moving over the land down towards rivers, lakes or the sea.

The **Himalayas** are a large mountain range in Asia, to the north of Bangladesh.

Severe flooding hits the Bangladeshi capital Dhaka.

Composition

The future is not entirely bleak for Bangladesh. Abdul is a twelve-year-old boy who lives in an area of Bangladesh which floods regularly. Read his school composition below, and find out about his good news.

GLOSSARY

Dhaka is the capital city of Bangladesh.

Kerosene is a type of fuel sometimes used for heating, also called paraffin.

The Best Day of My Life

I'm so excited! It was the first day of term today. Last year we couldn't get to school on a great many days because of the floods. Sometimes it was weeks. By the time I got back to school, I'd forgotten everything. It was very frustrating
5 because I want to study to be an architect when I'm older. If I miss school all the time, I will never succeed. Our father told us the situation was getting worse. He would often complain, saying, "We have no electricity and no cars and yet we suffer these terrible cyclones and storms caused by
10 the rich people in other countries."

But on this day of my life, everything was different. The best day: the school boat was coming! From now on it was going to come every day except Sunday and stay for three hours. My little sister, Maki, and I were ready an hour before
15 it was due to arrive. I held her hand tightly as we waited with all the other children at the edge of the water. We were all fizzing like bottles of lemonade and Maki was jumping up and down. She had missed much more school than I had. Our parents had been afraid to let her walk to school even
20 when it was open because of the dangerous water.

Bangladeshi children on a school boat.

Suddenly we could see the school boat gliding along the flood waters and we all cheered so loudly I'm sure they could have heard us in Dhaka! Although we all wanted to rush on board immediately it docked, we lined up as we were told and
25 walked on board respectfully. Oh, what a paradise met our eyes!

There were forty seats on the deck for us older children, and benches for twenty little ones in the bow. We had books and pens and there were even solar-powered computers and
30 a library for students older than us. The three hours passed so quickly that I could not believe it when it was time to go home again.

But the best was not yet over! We were each given a solar lamp to take home so we could do homework. Before, we could
35 never do any school work at home because our kerosene lamp was expensive to run, and it also polluted the air and made a nasty smell.

Now I really do believe I will be able to study and succeed and become an architect. Then I will design more boats for
40 our people, not just school and library boats, but for living in and for floating gardens where we could grow crops.

Comprehension

1 Describe some of the problems Abdul had with his schooling before the school boat was introduced.

2 What does Abdul's father blame on 'rich people in other countries'?

3 Why is the school boat particularly exciting for Maki?

4 Why do you think the three hours pass so quickly for Abdul?

5 What is the benefit of a 'solar lamp' for Abdul and his family?

Toolkit

The first *conditional* is used for talking about possibilities in the present or in the future. A first conditional sentence is made up of two clauses, an 'if' clause and a main clause.

Example: If you study hard, you will pass the test.

Looking closely

1 Which word or phrase could you use that means the same as 'suffer'? (paragraph 1)

2 Write down the simile used by Abdul in paragraph 2.

3 Which adverb tells you about the way the children went on board the school boat? (paragraph 3)

4 What does 'solar-powered' mean? (line 29)

5 Which word is the name of a kind of fuel? (paragraph 5)

Toolkit

 A *simile* is a comparison with two dissimilar things, using the words 'like' or 'as'.

Examples:
The snow lay *like* a blanket over the fields.

Her hair is *as* white *as* snow.

A *metaphor* goes one step further for poetic effect to make a direct statement (without using 'like' or 'as').

Example: A blanket of snow lay over the field.

Talking points

1 What are the main differences between your school and Abdul's?

2 Compare Abdul's views on school and education with your own. What are the similarities and differences?

Journal

Decribe a day at school that was exciting.

Identifying landscapes

The following pictures show different kinds of landscape from around the world. All of these landscapes are affected by changes in climate. Study the pictures and try to imagine the effect on each of them if temperatures were to rise by a significant amount.

- Match the following landscape words with the picture you think each fits: prairie, woodland, rain forest, desert, bush.
- In which countries might you find each of these different kinds of landscape?

Poem

One of the most devastating consequences of long spells of hot, dry weather is the potential for fires to start and spread rapidly. There are various causes of bush fires and forest fires. Some scientists believe that global warming is causing fiercer and more deadly fires. In the poem below Jackie Kay, who was brought up in Scotland, writes about a raging bush fire in Australia.

✄ Bush Fire ✄

That fire, they said, was red as red as red
as red as a fox, your lips, a cherry;
that fire, they said, spread and spread and spread,
faster than a cheetah or a nasty rumour;
5   that fire, they said, was hot, so hot, so hot,
hotter than lava or an African summer.

That fire, they said, was angry, very angry.
For three roaring days, it danced wildly, wildly, wildly.
Wild as flamenco, strip the willow, a Highland fling.
10   That fire, they said, had a big bad mouth,
swearing, spluttering, 'Bring it on! Bring it on!'

That fire, they said, wolfed down the lot –
the lovely little homes, the trees, the land.
That fire, they said, left nothing behind at all:
15   one blackened trail, one sad scorched story.

JACKIE KAY

Traditional Highland fling dancing.

Flamenco dancing.

Looking closely

1 With what does the writer compare the fire? Choose three comparisons and explain why they make the description more vivid.

2 How do the repeated 's' sounds add to the description of the fire?

3 What effect does the poem achieve with its personification of the fire?

4 Flamenco, strip-the-willow and the Highland fling are all very energetic dances. Why do you think these dances make appropriate comparisons for the raging fire?

5 What do you think the verb phrase 'to wolf down' means? (line 12)

Toolkit

The poem uses a variety of poetic techniques.

Personification is a type of metaphor. The fire is personified – made to seem like a human being; one that 'danced wildly', 'swearing, spluttering'.

Repetition is used throughout the poem for emphasis. For example, the first line says that the fire 'was red as red as red', to show how enormous and frightening the fire is becoming. **W**

Poetic description

From *Mukiwa* by Peter Godwin

The following extract is a description of a forest fire in South Africa.

ɘଠ ଉଇ

It was already gigantic when we arrived, a cavern of flame that soared ten storeys into the sky and blotted out the stars. A wall of intense heat blew off it and it was impossible to get anywhere near. The noise, too, was tremendous. Above the background roar, there were constant crashes as trees collapsed. Hundreds of birds wheeled about, calling in alarm at their destroyed nests and their lost young. And a barrage of wild animals came bowling out of the fire towards us, crazed by fear.

PETER GODWIN

Wordpool

cavern	barrage
storeys	bowling
intense	crazed
background	

Writing a poem

Write your own poem about some aspect of fire. Use these techniques to help you.

- In a small group, make a list of all the words you have read about fire and its effects. Think of other words that describe how fire can be seen, heard and felt.
- Make your words into vivid phrases. You could think of some metaphors of your own, like the fire's 'big bad mouth' in the poem, or the 'cavern of flame' in the description above. Or perhaps you could write something about fire that is more comforting.
- Now revise your phrases. You may take some ideas from others in your group to improve your own.
- Use your phrases to compose your own poem that describes the power of fire. W

Toolkit

A *simple metaphor* describes one thing in relation to another, like mixing temperature or the effects of weather conditions with people's moods and behaviour. *Examples*:
Cool it!
Hot head!

Think of other expressions that use heat, hot weather, or fire to describe human behaviour.

Weather forecasts

Do you ever listen to or read weather forecasts? Forecasting the weather has become an increasingly complex and scientific process. The results that weather scientists gather also provide information on issues like climate change. Forecasts are still only predictions, but what is certain is that the weather is very different around the world at any one time. Read the following weather forecasts for two different cities on 3 December 2008.

 Hot air is being funnelled over Southern Australia and bringing light showers. High pressure is bringing clear skies to the south-east. Temperatures today in Adelaide: 26°C to 30°C.

 Sunny spells but freezing fog will persist over north-east Scotland. Rain will move in and turn to snow overnight. Moderate to heavy falls of snow expected. Temperatures today in Aberdeen: 2°C to -3°C.

Wordpool

to funnel   overnight

pressure   moderate

to persist

Talking points

1 Why are these weather forecasts for the same day so different?

2 What is the weather usually like in your country in December?

Writing a weather forecast

Choose a place you know about or have lived in, and a particular month. Perhaps you could choose your favourite time of the year. Think about this month in terms of its typical weather patterns.

Add some personal touches to the script, and write it out as you would present it on television. **W**

3 Air

Who owns the air?

In this unit you will:

Experience	Read	Create
• Cuba	• poetry	• a class recital
• English and French paintings	• autobiography	• a description
• Glasgow	• an audio guide	• a poem
• Agra	• news articles	• an audio guide
• Zanzibar	• a ghost story	• a ghost story

> To one who has been long in city pent,
> 'Tis very sweet to look into the fair
> And open face of heaven.
>
> From 'To One Who Has Been Long in City Pent', John Keats, 1817

When you set off for school this morning, what kind of air did you breathe? What could you smell? In the quotation above, the nineteenth-century English poet John Keats describes the pleasure of being in the open air after spending a lot of time cooped up in the city of London.

GLOSSARY

Pent is a poetic word for *penned*, meaning shut up in a pen, or fenced enclosure.

'Tis is a poetic abbreviation for *It is*.

Cooped up is a modern way of saying *penned*.

Talking points

1 Think of the different kinds of air people breathe in different parts of the world. What is the difference between mountain air and sea air? What is the air like in big cities?

2 What do you think is the best kind of air?

Poem

The writer of the following poem, Nicolás Guillén, comes from Cuba. He believes that the air we breathe belongs to 'no one'. This means that we all share it and we should look after it. It is difficult to describe the feeling and movement of fresh air, but this poet has used words and images in an original way to try to capture its effects.

ಸಾ Can You? ಆ

Can you sell me the air that slips through your fingers,
strokes your face and tangles your hair?
Perhaps you could sell me five dollars' worth of wind,
or more, perhaps sell me a storm?
5 Perhaps you could sell me the delicate air
(not all of it) that dances
in your garden, from flower to flower,
dances in your garden among the birds,
ten dollars' worth of pure air?
10   The air spins and flits away
        Like a butterfly.
        No one owns it, no one.

Can you sell me some sky,
the sky that's sometimes blue
15 and sometimes grey,
a small strip of your sky,
the piece you think you bought with all the trees
in your orchard, as one buys the roof along with the house?
Can you sell me a dollar's worth
20 of sky, two miles
of sky, a slice of your sky,
whatever piece you can?
        The sky is high in the clouds.
        The clouds float by.
25   No one owns them, no one.

NICOLÁS GUILLÉN

This poem has been translated from the Spanish.

Wordpool

Discuss the meaning of the following words taken from the poem.

to stroke (line 2)
to tangle (2)
delicate (5)
among (8)
to flit (10)
orchard (18)

Make your own wordpool of any other unfamiliar words you come across.

1 How does the poet create a sense of what the air is like to touch and feel?

2 How does he describe the sky?

3 How does he contrast the freedom of the natural world with the human focus on making money?

4 What different images does the poet use to describe the sky?

Writers often use the repetition of sounds for poetic effect. This is called *alliteration*. You can use words that begin with the same sound, but often use different letters, like 's', 'sh' or 'z' to make a hissing or whispering sound (also known as *sibilance*).

1 How does it feel if the air 'slips through your fingers'? (line 1)

2 What is the poet trying to say by using the word 'dances'? (lines 6 and 8)

3 What is the effect of using the word 'perhaps' several times in the first stanza?

4 What do you think is suggested by the word 'flits'? (line 10)

Poetry recital

Poetry is often intended to be read aloud. Now you are going to present the poem 'Can You?' as a class recital.

- On a copy of the poem, highlight each question the poet has used in a different colour.
- Highlight the two three-line answers and the title in another colour.
- Discuss how the questions and answers should be spoken. For example, what happens to the tone of your voice when you ask a question?
- The whole class is then called upon to respond with the answer.

Practise your lines carefully! How does hearing the poem read out aloud help you understand it better?

What is fresh air like?

Do you enjoy being in the countryside and breathing in fresh air? Do you like looking up at the clouds? Do you think it is possible to create an image of the wind in the sky?

Before the invention of photography, English painters like John Constable were interested in trying to capture the changeable effects of light and weather.

Landscape with Grey Windy Sky, by John Constable, painted in 1821–30.

Writing a description

Write a description of what it would be like to be crossing this field.

- Describe the sights, sounds and smells of the air.
- Make it sound real by starting out with a reason for why you might be there. Are you taking a shortcut on your way home?

Looking closely

1 What do you think the air is like in this painting?

2 Describe the weather in this painting.

3 How has the artist created the effect of wind and the movement of the clouds?

4 How quickly do you think Constable painted this picture?

What is it like to live in polluted air?

Prose fiction

From *Bleak House* by Charles Dickens

In the opening chapter of his famous novel *Bleak House,* the English writer Charles Dickens describes the thick fog that sometimes descended on London in the 1830s.

๛ Fog ๛

Smoke lowering down from chimney-pots, making a soft black drizzle with flakes of soot in it as big as full-grown snow flakes … Fog everywhere. Fog up the river … fog down the river … fog in the eyes and throats of old men wheezing by their firesides … people peeping over the bridges into a sky of fog, with fog all round them, as if they were up in a balloon, and hanging in the misty clouds.

CHARLES DICKENS

Wordpool

to drizzle

soot

to wheeze

fascinating

strangely

Toolkit

Dickens' novels are full of lively descriptions of people and places. He uses *noun phrases* made up of one or more words that accompany the noun. These may be a series of adjectives or a determiner (an article or another word that indicates quantity).

Example: a soft black drizzle

This London fog was thick and harmful because of the pollution from burning coal and wood used in people's homes and workshops. But some artists, such as Claude Monet, liked to paint its fascinating effects. Have you ever thought that the effects of pollution can be beautiful? On the following page is Monet's 1899 picture of *Parliament in the Fog* showing the Houses of Parliament at Westminster in a strangely dark and colourful light.

Parliament in theFog painted by Claude Monet in 1899.

Looking closely

1   Describe the painting to a partner.

2   What do you think of the strange effects created by the artist's use of light and colour?

3   What do you think it would feel like to be in a fog like this?

Talking points

1   Do you know of a place where the air is unpleasant or harmful?

2   Can pollution kill you?

3   Is all pollution visible?

4   How important do you think clean air is?

Autobiography

From *Tales from the Back Green* by Bill Paterson

It was not just London which suffered these terrible fogs. Here the writer Bill Paterson remembers his childhood in the 1950s in Glasgow, Scotland. Until 1962 the city of Glasgow had trams that ran on tracks in the roads.

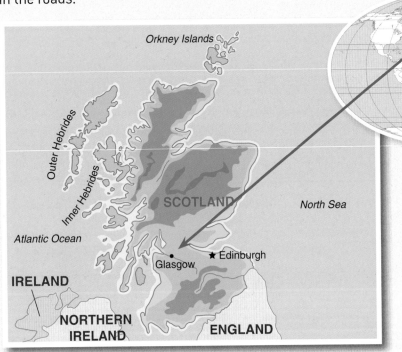

Map of Scotland and the British Isles showing the location of Glasgow.

Wordpool

cancelled [line 6]

indoor [8]

vehicles [10]

to creep [13]

zones [21]

GLOSSARY

A **swimming gala** is a special event where pupils compete against each other, or another school, in swimming. What word would you use in your language?

Respiratory is a clinical (medical) term that describes the function of breathing.

Murk means a gloomy darkness. The adjective 'murky' is more commonly used than the noun 'murk'.

◇ Glasgow Fog ◇

And then there was the fog. It wasn't only London that had deep and dirty fogs in those days. Glasgow had some really thick ones when you couldn't see your hand in front of your face. I once walked into a lamp-post on my way to the school
5 swimming gala. When I got to the swimming baths an hour later they had cancelled it. It had not been cancelled for respiratory health reasons, but because you couldn't see one end of the indoor pool from the other.

When fog like that came down, the city trams were the only
10 vehicles which could move. They were the only things sure

of where they were going. The city was already fixed beneath their wheels. Solid on their steel tracks, and lit from end to end, they crept along like ghostly ships. For most of the year, the car, bus and lorry drivers thought the slow-moving trams

15   were a nuisance. But when the smog came down, they followed the trams like ducklings following their mother.

'What number's that?' an unseen car driver would call out from the murk.

'It's an 8!' the conductor would call back.

20   The car driver would then follow the tram, knowing that he would make it into town. In the end the smokeless zones cleared the fogs, and the buses and cars brought an end to the trams.

BILL PATERSON

Comprehension

1   Why was the swimming gala cancelled?

2   Explain what the writer means when he says about the trams, 'The city was already fixed beneath their wheels'.

3   Usually car drivers found the trams a nuisance. Why did they change their minds when it was foggy?

Looking closely

1   Write down two similes from the text. (You looked at a simile in unit 2, on page 36.) Explain the comparison the writer makes in each one.

2   Smog is made up of two words joined together. Can you work out what the two words are?

What problems come from polluted air?

The Taj Mahal

Have you heard of the Taj Mahal in Agra, India? Maybe you have even been to see it. It is a magnificent collection of buildings erected on the orders of the Mughal Emperor Shah Jahan following the death of his wife in 1631. Look at the image below and read the audio guide transcript.

> **GLOSSARY**
>
> A **transcript** is the written copy or script.
>
> **Inlaid** means inserted into the hollowed-out space of carved wood or stone.
>
> **Calligraphy** means beautiful writing. It is often used to refer to script drawn with a brush.
>
> A **mosque** is a Muslim place of worship.
>
> A **guest house** is a place where visitors can stay.

Welcome! You are standing at the main gateway of the Taj Mahal, the tomb of Emperor Shah Jehan's wife Mumtaz Mahal. Her name means 'beloved ornament of the palace', and you will see how much ornament has been created in her honour. This gateway is a magnificent structure in itself, designed to impress you. It is nearly 100 feet high, and 150 feet wide, and made from red sandstone. Please walk inside.

As you can see, no expense has been spared in the detail, as in these floral forms that are made of marble inlaid with precious stones. This very skilful work is still done by hand in workshops in Agra today. The heavy door that you walk through is made up of eight different metals. Please notice the beautiful calligraphy of the black marble quotations from the Quran. Now, walk through to see the beautifully planned garden. On your left is a mosque and to your right is a guest house. Straight ahead is the tomb itself. From this distance it looks small, but as we get closer you will see that it is colossal in size …

Restoring the Taj Mahal

The original marble of the Taj Mahal has been discoloured by air pollution and a great deal of restoration work is now underway. The article below describes what is being done.

INDIA MINISTRY OF TOURISM, 21 JANUARY 2008

Taj Mahal's Walls to Receive Some TLC

ICONIC MARBLE TO GET UNIQUE RESTORATIVE TREATMENT

It's one of the most iconic buildings in the world, but time and pollution have taken their toll. So from this week the Taj Mahal is getting a unique restorative beauty treatment of its own.

Over the years, an accumulation of dust and other pollution from the industrial city of Agra has stained its walls yellow.

Now those famous white marble walls will be coated in Multani mitti, or fuller's earth – a type of clay that's usually used in face masks and other body treatments.

The clay is left on overnight and then removed as soon as it begins to dry.

The treatments will be applied until March 2008 and will be repeated for another three months early in 2009. However, the monument will remain open as normal throughout the work – hopefully looking more sensational than ever.

GLOSSARY

TLC stands for 'tender loving care'.

Iconic comes from the word for an image of worship. It is also used to describe a significant example of art or architecture from a particular period in history.

A **face mask** is a covering of creams and other ingredients applied to the face to clean or smooth the skin.

Wordpool

restorative

accumulation

industrial

Fuller's earth

treatment

sensational

monument

Part of the Taj Mahal's inlaid marble.

Modern inlaid marble made in Agra.

Comprehension

1 What is remarkable about the main gateway to the Taj Mahal?

2 What does the audio guide describe as being on your left and right as you walk through the main gateway?

3 What kind of clay is being used to clean the marble of the Taj Mahal?

4 When does the news article say the work is taking place?

An audio guide map of the Taj Mahal

Below is a map of the Taj Mahal, showing the location of the audio guide 'hot spots', where listeners can select a number to listen to a recorded commentary.

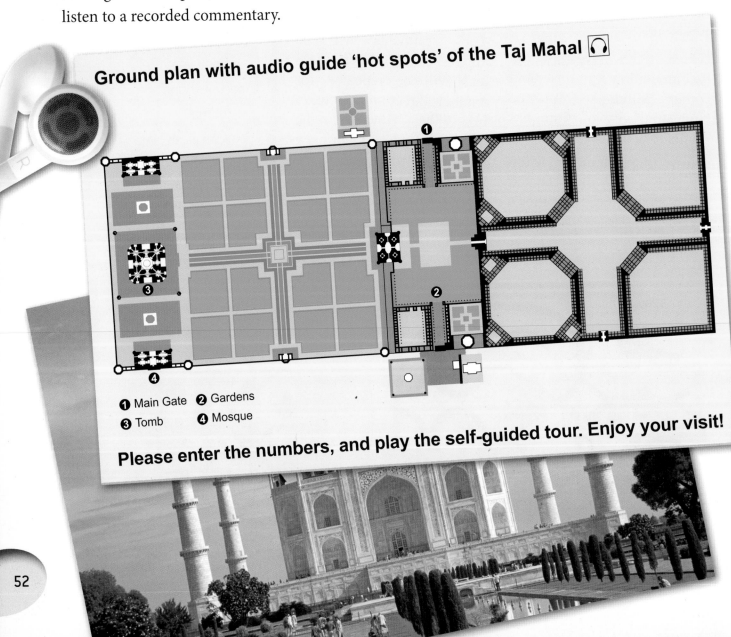

Ground plan with audio guide 'hot spots' of the Taj Mahal

❶ Main Gate ❷ Gardens
❸ Tomb ❹ Mosque

Please enter the numbers, and play the self-guided tour. Enjoy your visit!

Writing an audio guide

An audio guide is a recorded commentary about the things in a museum, or the history of a place of interest. Visitors can listen to them as they walk around. An audio tour gives information about the history of a place and other background details.

- Write the script for an audio guide about a place of interest you have visited. It could be a historical building, town landmark or even your school and grounds.
- Read the example on the Taj Mahal for ideas.
- Read your audio guide to the class and see if they can guess where it is.
- Make a map leaflet to accompany your guide, and include the 'hot spots' marked with an audio guide icon. [W]

Prose fiction

The following text is a ghost story from Zanzibar. There is no pollution, but something different in the air!

❧ Something in the Air ❧

Suleiman was feeling happy, but a little anxious. He had just sold his last mango in the market. It was a good season this year and his fruit had sold well, but how long would this last? The sun was blazing down as usual as he counted his
5 money, zipped it inside his pouch and prepared to mount his bicycle for the journey home. Just as he took hold of the handlebars, he saw a man walking purposefully towards him. The man was wearing long, white Arab dress and a neat white cap.

10 'Asslaamu alaykum,' the stranger said politely.

Suleiman barely had time to respond with 'Wa alaykum salaam' before the man placed his hands on the handlebars and continued, 'Suleiman, I have a job for you tomorrow, if you will do it.'

15 Amazed that the stranger knew his name, Suleiman looked at him. Suddenly he felt a cool draught of air and noticed that the man's light robe billowed on this hot, windless day.

'Don't be alarmed,' the stranger continued. 'I will pay you
20 more for a day's work than you would earn in a year. I know you are the best mango picker in Zanzibar and I want you to harvest my mangoes. That is all. Will you meet me tomorrow morning at Mnazi Mmoja at seven o'clock? I will take you to my mango orchard.'

25 Suleiman stood dumbfounded and was just about to question the stranger when he disappeared into the bustle of the market. The cool draught had vanished along with the finely dressed man. Suleiman stood motionless for a few minutes, dazed by what had happened.

GLOSSARY

Asslaamu alaykum is an Arabic greeting meaning 'Peace be upon you'. The traditional reply is *Wa alaykum salaam*, meaning 'And upon you be peace'.

A **draught** is a current or stream of cool air.

Someone who is **dumbfounded** is so surprised that he or she cannot speak.

Wordpool

anxious (line 1)

to blaze (4)

to billow (17)

to harvest (22)

intense (47)

succulent (54)

30   Next morning, after a restless night, he wondered if he had dreamed it all.

'You may as well go to meet him,' said his wife. 'There are no mangoes to sell today – you have nothing to lose.'

So Suleiman set off on his bicycle. It was an hour's ride to Mnazi
35   Mmoja. When he arrived there was no mango orchard to be seen, but the stranger in white Arab dress was waiting for him. As Suleiman propped his bicycle against a tree, the man approached him, and Suleiman again felt the cool draught. He shivered and saw the fine white robe billowing in the sudden wind. A moment
40   later, the robe was perfectly still. The man smiled and greeted him politely, as before.

'Come with me and I will take you to my orchard, Suleiman,' he said.

Suleiman greeted his employer and untied his baskets, which
45   contained his ropes and large sharp knife, from his bicycle. After they had walked a few yards, Suleiman was about to ask where the mango orchard was when he was overwhelmed by an intense perfume. Everything went black for a moment. When he opened his eyes again he found himself in the greenest and most beautiful
50   orchard of mango trees he had ever seen.

'I will return at sunset,' said the stranger with a smile, and suddenly he was gone.

Suleiman started picking the fruit. They were wonderfully ripe. They smelled more sweetly and were more succulent than any
55   mango he had seen in all his forty years. By sunset he had made a huge pile. There were more mangoes than he could possibly count.

At sunset the man returned. He was pleased with Suleiman's work and pressed his wages into his hand. It was just as he had
60   promised: more money than Suleiman could hope to earn in a year. Suleiman picked up his baskets and ropes and was putting his knife away carefully in his pouch, with the money, when he felt the cool draught. He looked up. The man had disappeared.

The intense perfume which had overwhelmed him in the morning
65 suddenly enveloped him and again, everything was instantly black. When he opened his eyes, he was standing under the tree by his bicycle. There was no sign of the mango orchard.

He tied his baskets onto his bicycle and started the long ride home. On his return his wife and little children gathered round
70 him.

'Was he there? What happened?' asked his wife.

'I do not know,' answered Suleiman and, feeling suddenly weak, he leaned against the table, and told his wife his tale.

When he finished the story, with trembling hands he took off
75 his pouch, unsure whether the money, too, would prove to be some kind of dream. But there it was, and when his wife saw it she danced around the house with the children.

Comprehension

1 What surprises Suleiman about the stranger when he first approaches?

2 What is so special about the stranger's mango orchard?

3 What does Suleiman experience before and after he works in the stranger's orchard?

4 How does Suleiman feel when he returns to his home?

5 Why does Suleiman's wife dance around the house?

Looking closely

1 What does the adverb 'purposefully' tell you about the way the stranger approaches Suleiman? (line 7)

2 Which word could replace 'barely'? (line 11)

3 What does the word 'intense' tell you about the way the perfume smelled? (line 47)

4 Make a list of the words used to describe the stranger's mangoes.

5 Rewrite the sentence 'There was no sign of the mango orchard' using different words to say the same thing. (line 67)

Writing a ghost story

Have you heard stories of strange, unexplained things happening or 'things going bump in the night'? This is what ghost stories are often about. They don't necessarily include an actual ghost, but they are about something unusual that cannot be explained.

- Write your own ghost story. You can make it up entirely. If you base it on a story you have heard in the past, try to give it an original twist of your own.
- Use the story *Something in the Air* as a model to guide you: include direct speech, and descriptions of the strange experiences or events that occur.
- Alternatively, write a new ending to the story *Something in the Air*. Use a mixture of ordinary words and very descriptive passages to emphasize the strange events. W

Toolkit

Comparative adjectives and adverbs are used to compare things. They are shown by an added -er at the end of an adjective, or using the word 'more' in front of an adjective or an adverb.

Superlatives are used to describe the most extreme version of something, by adding -est at the end of an adjective, or putting the word 'most' in front of an adjective or adverb.

Example: 'the greenest and most beautiful orchard'.

Catastrophe!

4

What happens under the Earth's plates?

In this unit you will:

Experience
- the Bay of Naples in 79 CE
- Thailand
- English, Japanese and Norwegian paintings

Read
- a web page
- diagrams
- a letter
- prose non-fiction

Create
- a reconstructed text
- a radio report
- a role-play

Forests were set on fire … and the crackling trunks
Extinguished with a crash – and all was black.

From 'Darkness' by Lord Byron, 1816

The dark summer of 1816

Can you imagine how you would feel if all was complete darkness, day and night? Can you imagine not being able to see the sun, the moon or the stars? This is what people experienced after the Tambora volcano erupted in Indonesia in 1815.

About 80,000 people on two Indonesian islands were killed. The results of the eruption were catastrophic. The eruption released dust into the Earth's atmosphere, blotting out the sun. Temperatures were reduced across the whole planet. It was a year of very poor harvests and a shortage of food because crops could not grow. Because of this, 1816 was known in Europe as the 'year without a summer'.

Poem

It was this dark summer of 1816 that the English poet Lord Byron described in his poem *Darkness* in the opening quotation. Here are some more lines from the same poem.

ೞ **Darkness** ೞ

I had a dream, which was not all a dream.
The bright sun was extinguished, and the stars
Did wander darkling in the eternal space,
Rayless, and pathless, and the icy Earth
Swung blind and blackening in the moonless air;
Morn came and went – and came, and brought no day.

GLOSSARY

Darkling is an old-fashioned and rare word. It is a poetic way of saying 'in the dark'.

Rayless is used by Byron to emphasize the fact that the rays of light from the stars could no longer be seen on Earth because of the dust.

Wordpool

Discuss the meaning of the following words taken from the poem.

to crackle

trunk

to extinguish

eternal

blind

Make your own wordpool of any other unfamiliar words you come across.

Word origins

'Catastrophe' comes from the ancient Greek word *katastrophe* meaning 'a sudden turning'. Today, we have come to apply the word to all natural disasters caused by earthquakes, tidal waves, forest fires, and volcanoes.

What is a volcano?

Web page

What do you know about volcanoes? The introduction below from the How Stuff Works website describes what people tend to think of when they imagine a volcano.

How Volcanoes Work

Every so often you hear about a major volcanic eruption somewhere in the world. Of course, there are many news stories that cover the event or catastrophe. People throughout history have been in awe of the sight or description of a raging violent volcano. How can a quiet, peaceful mountain suddenly become a terrifying and transforming force?

So what is a volcano? Under the earth's crust or surface is the mantle which is made up of extremely hot rock. When the earth's plates move away or towards each other, it can cause the mantle to melt and move around. Sometimes the melted mantle or magma fills in gaps under the earth's crust. If there is no room, the magma can be forced out of the earth's crust to form a volcano. Sometimes a volcano can happen under the ocean. Sometimes the magma will spread out along the bottom of the ocean and spew out magma above the surface of the water.

www.howstuffworks.com

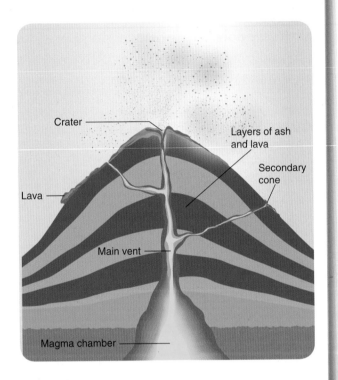

Crater

Layers of ash and lava

Secondary cone

Lava

Main vent

Magma chamber

Wordpool

awe

transforming

mantle

crust

spew

GLOSSARY

Magma is fluid molten rock.

Earth's plates are huge sections of the earth's crust that move around. The plates are from 50 to 250 miles thick.

Talking points

1 Look at the diagram and take turns to explain to each other the parts of the volcano.

2 Does the diagram help you to understand how volcanoes work?

3 What does it mean to be 'in awe' of the destructive power of nature?

4 Name some volcanoes from different countries.

The eruption of Mount Vesuvius, 79 CE

Mount Vesuvius is situated in the Bay of Naples in Italy. It is one of the most active volcanoes in the world, yet 3,000,000 people live close to it. Its most recent eruption was in 1944. Its most famous and catastrophic eruption, in 79 CE, resulted in the destruction of the Roman cities of Pompeii and Herculaneum. The remains of these cities are visited by thousands of people every year.

There is a vivid description of the eruption in the letter of a Roman known as Pliny the Younger. In these letters he describes his uncle, Pliny the Elder, trying to save people on the other side of the Bay of Naples, close to the eruption. The following text is part of a description of the events of that night. Pliny's description of the eruption was so detailed that scientists who study volcanoes named a type of eruption, the 'Plinian', after him.

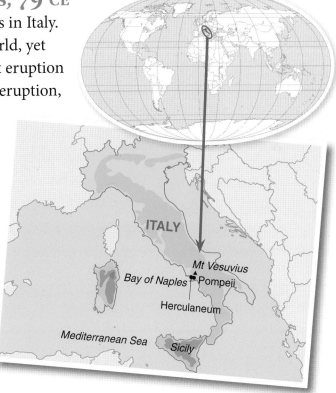

The location of Mount Vesuvius in Italy.

Reconstructing a text

The text written by Pliny the Younger is over the page, but you must not look at it until you have completed this task! First, your teacher will play a recording of the text to you.

- As your teacher reads the text for the first time, listen carefully.
- While your teacher reads it for the second time, you may take some brief notes.
- Then, in a small group, reconstruct the text by writing out what you remember as carefully as you can. **W**

My uncle Pliny ordered ships to be made ready and they set out across the bay. He was anxious to save as many of the people living at the foot of Vesuvius as he could. It was a great adventure to him as he was a keen scientist and he could observe the changing shapes and colours of the great cloud. Ash was now falling onto the ships.

As they drew closer to land, the atmosphere became darker and denser. Pieces of rock burned and blackened by the fire landed on the ships' decks. The sea was so thick with debris that they could not approach the land. So they sailed to the other side of the bay and into the harbour. Ships there were ready to evacuate the inhabitants, but were trapped by the wind, unable to escape. Broad sheets of brilliant flame were now lighting up many parts of the mountain as my uncle and his men hurried into a nearby house. Its floors rose and fell as ash and stone flowed beneath them. Then it was rocked by strong tremors and began to slide.

Outside was also dangerous as ash and pieces of rock rained down. Pliny and the group of terrified people tied pillows to their heads and set out back to the ships in a shower of rocks. Elsewhere it was daybreak, but here was darkness thicker and blacker than any night. By the light of their torches, they succeeded in reaching the ships. But the water was so rough and thick with debris that they could not sail.

PLINY THE YOUNGER

Comprehension

1 What did Pliny the Elder hope to achieve by making the dangerous journey to Mount Vesuvius during the eruption?

2 What changes did Pliny observe as he got closer to the land?

3 Why do you think the people were tying pillows to their heads?

4 What stopped Pliny and the others escaping by boat?

Wordpool

debris	ash
harbour	tremors
evacuate	torches
brilliant	

What is a volcano like?

Many artists have tried to capture the violence and force of a volcano erupting. Below are two examples by the Norwegian painter Johan Christian Dahl and the English artist Joseph Wright of Derby. Joseph Wright painted over 30 paintings of Mount Vesuvius after he saw an eruption in 1773–5. He was fascinated by the dramatic and colourful effects of fire at night, and used the subject of a volcano erupting to experiment with light effects.

Eruption of Vesuvius by Johan Christian Dahl, painted in 1828.

Vesuvius in Eruption, with a View over the Islands in the Bay of Naples, by Joseph Wright of Derby, painted in 1776–80.

The next picture is very different. It is a print of Mount Fuji by the Japanese artist Katsushika Hokusai. In 1827, Hokusai began work on a series of 36 woodblock prints of Mount Fuji.

Mount Fuji, which last erupted in 1707, is one of Japan's Three Holy Mountains, and is celebrated for the unusually perfect shape of its cone. When conditions are right, in late summer or early autumn, with a wind from the south and a clear sky, the slopes of Mount Fuji can appear red from the rays of the sun.

South Wind, Clear Sky (also known as *Red Fuji*), a woodblock print by Katsushika Hokusai.

Producing a radio report

You should have plenty of vivid and dramatic phrases and useful words in your wordpool by now. Use these to write a radio report about witnessing an eruption of Mount Vesuvius. As you are one of the first reporters at the scene, you will need to describe what you can see and explain what is happening for the listeners. Make the facts sound exciting.

Fact: Hot lava flows down the side of the volcano.

Description: The lava is like a red river of burning rocks. The heat and smoke is so intense, it is impossible to get close to it.

- Write several of these pairs of facts and descriptions to help you draft the report. Use the new vocabulary you have learned in this unit.
- Make sure your report is clearly worded. Aim to include plenty of factual detail and vivid descriptions.
- Read your report aloud, or record it to hear how it sounds. Practise the way you say it out loud to make it sound exciting.
- Use direct and indirect speech to report what other experts and witnesses have to say about it.

Toolkit

When you are focusing on describing one particular thing in detail, you often need to make use of a wide range of synonyms. *Synonyms* are words that have the same, or nearly the same, meanings. For example, in describing volcanoes, you might need a range of synonyms to express the great power of an eruption, such as: 'terrible', 'fearful', or 'awe-inspiring'.

What causes earthquakes and tsunamis?

Do you know what causes earthquakes? When one of the Earth's plates slips under another at a plate boundary, it can create an earthquake. These plate boundaries are called fault lines. Cities built on fault lines are at risk of earthquakes.

When an earthquake occurs under the ocean, the tremendous energy of the earthquake is transferred to the water. Waves travel under the oceans faster than a jet plane. These waves can be hundreds of miles long and over 10 metres high. When they reach the shore, the effect is a devastating *tsunami*.

This is what happened on 26 December 2004, when a gigantic earthquake occurred underwater, off the coast of Sumatra in Indonesia. It caused a tsunami which covered 600 kilometres in 75 minutes. The tsunami caused devastation. A great many people lost their lives, and many communities were destroyed across Southeast Asia.

Word origin

Tsunami is a Japanese word from *tsu* meaning 'harbour' and *nami* meaning 'wave'.

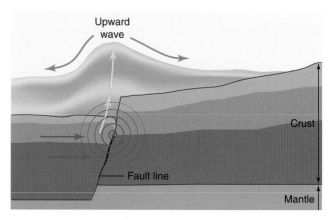

How a tsunami is created.

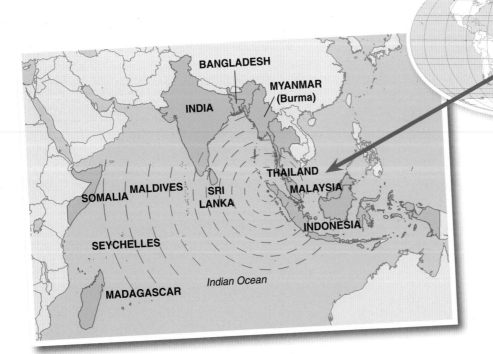

Map of the region most affected by the 2004 tsunami, showing the epicentre of the earthquake.

Interpreting images

The Great Wave off Kanagawa by Katsushika Hokusai.

Scene in India following the 2004 tsunami.

Image 1 was created by the same Japanese artist who made the print of Mount Fuji that you looked at earlier. You can see Mount Fuji in the background, but the main part of the picture is a giant wave, or tsunami, at Kanagawa in Japan.

Image 2 shows the devastation caused by the 2004 tsunami and its impact on people's lives.

Looking closely

1 What do these images make you feel about tsunamis and their effects?

2 Why do you think the artist and the photographer made the images they did?

3 What images come into your mind when you think of the word catastrophe?

Prose non-fiction

The following text is the true story of Ningnong. She is an elephant who used to give rides to children on one of the beaches hit by the tsunami in Thailand in 2004.

❧ **Ningnong's Great Day** ☙

Yong was very proud of his young she-elephant, Ningnong. She was strong and good-tempered and never tired of her work. Every morning Yong rose early and rode Ningnong down to the beach. This was Yong's favourite time of day as
5 he watched the waves breaking on the white sand, and breathed in the beauty of the place he loved. The tourists had not yet arrived, and the beach belonged to Yong and his elephant.

On this morning, 26 December 2004, Yong had no idea of
10 the catastrophe which would soon engulf far more than the coast of Thailand. He did not know, either, that not far away the elephants at a tourist centre had spent a restless night, pulling at their chains. Oblivious to all this, Yong watched the birds swirling over the turquoise water in the bay until
15 he heard the excited cries of the children as the first tourists arrived on the beach. Soon a child would ask for a ride on the elephant, and Ningnong's working day would begin.

The day went on like any other day as Ningnong plodded up and down the hot sand and splashed through the shallow
20 water with children on her back. Yong did not know that at the tourist centre above the beach, the elephants had succeeded in breaking their chains and had run up the hill away from the beach. The owners knew something was wrong, and along with some Japanese tourists, they had followed the
25 elephants inland away from the beach.

Suddenly Yong became aware that something strange was happening. The water was disappearing. It seemed as though some gigantic force was sucking it away. The tourists had noticed it, too. Some were running away up the beach, and

30 some ran down the beach to see what was happening. Ningnong started to stamp her great feet and make strange noises. Suddenly the air was filled with a low roaring noise. As it grew louder, Ningnong pulled at her ropes. In horror and disbelief, people stared at the wall of water which was approaching the beach.

35 How could any wave be that vast? And how could it travel so fast?

There was panic all around Yong. People were shouting and screaming and trying to run with children in their arms. Yong held tight onto the terrified child already riding with him as

40 Ningnong tried to break into a run. Another little girl stood at Ningnong's feet, screaming in terror.

'Oom kun!' ('Pick up!') cried Yong.

Ningnong lifted up the child with her trunk, and having placed her beside Yong, she broke into a run. She raced up the

45 beach and the hillside to safety. Unlike hundreds of people on the beach that day, she and her riders escaped the deadly tsunami which caused such terrible devastation.

1 Why do you think early morning was Yong's favourite time of day?

2 Write down a synonym for engulf. (line 10)

3 The colour turquoise is a mixture of blue and green (line 14). Write down as many words as you can for different shades of the colours blue and green.

4 Ningnong plodded up and down the beach (line 18). What kind of movement is 'plodding'?

5 Explain what you think the people were feeling when they stared 'in horror and disbelief'. (line 33)

Role-playing an interview

Work in a small group to produce a role-play based on the story of Yong and the little girl Ningnong picked up with her trunk. One of you will play the part of Yong, and another the girl who was saved. One or more other members of the group will take the role of a journalist recording an interview for a television news programme.

- If you are playing the part of the journalist, prepare questions to ask Yong and the girl.
- If you are playing the part of Yong or the little girl, re-read the story to remember details and understand the feelings involved.
- When you carry out the interview, you can use details from the text or make up extra information that fits the story. **W**

Word search

- See how many words connected to the topic in this unit you can find in this word search grid. Use a photocopied sheet, not your book!

- With a different coloured highlighter pen, find and colour in six words running across the grid.

- With a different colour, highlight the eight words running down the grid.

- Some letters will be shared and have two colours on them, so choose colours which mix well together.

E	A	R	T	H	Q	U	A	K	E
R	C	V	O	S	C	R	U	S	T
U	O	L	A	C	T	I	V	E	U
P	L	A	V	O	S	B	B	C	R
T	L	V	O	N	U	R	N	C	Q
I	I	A	L	E	N	I	A	R	U
O	D	E	C	M	A	G	M	A	O
N	E	F	A	L	M	M	G	T	I
P	V	E	N	T	I	T	H	E	S
A	T	M	O	S	P	H	E	R	E

5 Feeding the world

How can we make sure that there is enough food for everyone?

In this unit you will:

Experience
- Korea
- Brazil
- Malawi
- French, Italian and Dutch paintings

Read
- a Portrait of the Week
- prose fiction
- a web advertisement
- a travel diary
- a poem

Create
- a Painting of the Week
- diary entries
- a poem

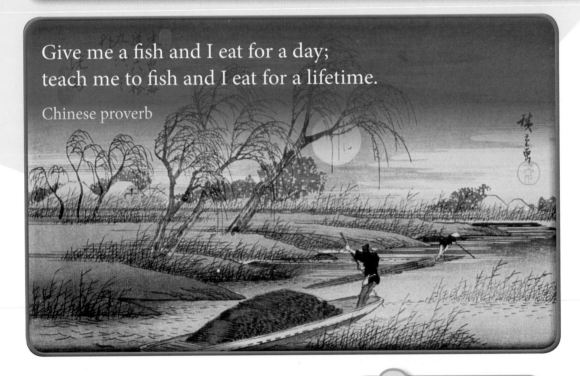

Give me a fish and I eat for a day;
teach me to fish and I eat for a lifetime.

Chinese proverb

The world we live in has abundant and varied things for people to eat. There are thousands upon thousands of fruits, vegetables, meats, fish, spices, herbs and grains which humans enjoy eating. Many people work hard to farm the land, tend to livestock and fish the seas, yet the world does not manage to provide enough food for everyone.

Talking points

1 What do you think the Chinese proverb above means?

2 What do you think it must be like to have hardly any food?

3 Why do you think some people in the world do not have enough to eat?

Portrait of the Week

This picture was painted by the Italian artist Giuseppe Arcimboldo in 1573. He has created something that is part portrait, and part still-life painting! How many fruits, vegetables and other foods can you see in it? Read one person's imaginative description of this painting below. It was written for a series called 'Portrait of the Week' in a newspaper.

Summer by Giuseppe Arcimboldo.

This is someone and no one. The dark space of his eyes reveals an emptiness within his shell of summer fruits that is disconcerting and eerie. He is a freak, a chimera. Constructed of wheat, figs, plums, pomegranates, peaches, pears and melon, this is like an image from a folk song or sinister tale – the king of summer whose fate is to be burnt at the end of August in some savage rite.

Jonathan Jones, *The Guardian*, 'Portrait of the Week No. 72'

Wordpool

Discuss the meaning of the following words taken from the extract on this page.

emptiness

to disconcert

eerie

freak

sinister

fate

savage

Make your own wordpool of any other unfamiliar words you come across.

Still-life painting

Study the two still-life paintings below. The first was painted by the Dutch artist Floris van Dijck in 1615–20. The second, by French artist Paul Cézanne, was painted in 1890–94. The still-life tradition in the Netherlands in the seventeenth century was part of the Christian tradition of the *vanitas*, with its focus on the fragility of earthly life. Later images are more of a celebration of the fruits of the harvest, and of country life.

Still Life with Cheeses by Floris van Dijck.

 Looking closely

1 Can you name all the different foods in the paintings?

2 What is the difference in the painting style and the way the food and objects are arranged? What is similar about them?

3 Compare and contrast the use of colour and the effects of light and shade. What kind of mood do these effects create?

Still life with a Basket of Apples by Paul Cézanne.

Writing your own Painting of the Week

Reread the 'Portrait of the Week' about Arcimboldo's *Summer*. You are now going to write about your own Painting of the Week. Choose one of the paintings illustrated on these pages and write a paragraph about it.

- Describe the painted scene in vivid detail.
- How life-like is the scene?
- Do you feel like you are part of the picture?
- What is the overall mood of the painting?
- Begin with a catchy phrase, as if you are writing a story.

Toolkit

Nouns can be modified with additional words placed before or after the noun. These phrases can include additional nouns, adverbs and adjectives to provide descriptive detail and emotional expression. **W**

Examples from the 'Portraits of the Week':

- 'The dark space of his **eyes**'
- 'his shell of summer **fruits**'. **W**

What is it like not to have enough to eat?

Look at this photograph of people picking over a rubbish heap, searching for anything that could be used or sold for food.

People looking for things to re-use or sell on a rubbish heap.

When you were discussing hunger, did you think about pictures you may have seen on television of people starving in countries suffering from famine? Perhaps you talked about how drought has destroyed farmers' crops and created food shortages. But did you think of people who do not have enough to eat in some of the world's biggest modern cities?

It is usually animals that *forage*, or search for food, but when people are desperately hungry, they too forage in rubbish bins or anywhere they may find something edible. What do you think life must be like for these people?

Prose fiction

From *A Single Shard* by Linda Sue Park

The following text comes from a story set in a village in Korea in the twelfth century. Tree-ear is a twelve-year-old boy who shares a shelter under a bridge with Crane-man, a kindly old man who has looked after Tree-ear since he was a very young orphan. He called Tree-ear by that name because he was an orphan and had no parents, just like tree-ear, a wrinkly fungus which seems to just emerge from rotten wood. Both Crane-man and Tree-ear are constantly hungry and survive on what they can forage.

Tree-ear fungus.

✁ A Lucky Day ✃

Tree-ear was setting off in the early morning to forage in the village rubbish heaps. Ahead of him a man carried a heavy load on a jiggeh, an open-framed backpack made of branches. On the jiggeh was a large container made of woven straw,
5 the kind commonly used to carry rice.

Tree-ear knew that the rice must be from last-year's crop; in the fields surrounding the village this season's rice had only just begun to grow. It would be many months before the rice was harvested and the poor people allowed to glean the fallen
10 grain from the bare fields. Only then would they taste the rice and feel its solid goodness in their bellies. Just looking at the man's backpack made Tree-ear even hungrier.

Then, as Tree-ear stared, rice began to trickle out. The trickle thickened and became a stream. Oblivious to the hole in his
15 straw container, the man continued on his way.

For a few short moments Tree-ear's thoughts wrestled with one another. Tell him – quickly! Before he loses too much. No! Don't say anything – you will be able to pick up the fallen rice after he rounds the bend …

20 Tree-ear made his decision. He waited until the man had reached the bend in the road, then ran to catch him up.

'Honourable sir,' Tree-ear said, panting and bowing. 'As I walked behind you, I noticed that you are losing rice from your jiggeh!'

25 The farmer turned and saw the trail of rice. He pushed his straw hat back, scratched his head, and laughed ruefully.

'Impatience!' said the farmer. 'I should have had a double wall in this container. But it would have taken more time. Now I am paying for not having waited a little longer.'

30 He struggled out of the jiggeh's straps and inspected the container. He prodded the straw to close the gap, but without success.

Wordpool

container [line 4]

glean [9]

oblivious [14]

temporary [34]

dignity [47]

'Fetch me a few leaves, boy,' said the farmer. Tree-ear did so, and the man stuffed them into the container as a temporary
35   patch.

The farmer squatted down to load the jiggeh onto his back. As he started walking, he called over his shoulder. 'One good deed deserves another, boy. The rice on the ground is yours.'

40   'Many thanks, kind sir!' Tree-ear bowed, very pleased. His waist-pouch would soon be filled with rice.

Tree-ear had learned from Crane-man's example. Foraging in the woods and rubbish heaps and gathering fallen grain-heads in the autumn required time and work. They were
45   honourable ways to gather food. But stealing and begging made a man no better than a dog.

'Work gives a man dignity, stealing takes it away,' Crane-man had often said.

LINDA SUE PARK

Comprehension

1 What is the pack on the man's back made of?

2 Why are poor people like Tree-ear hungry at this time of year?

3 In what way is the man 'paying for not having waited a little longer'? (line 29)

4 What does the saying 'One good deed deserves another' mean? (lines 37 and 38)

5 What does Tree-ear believe is the difference between 'foraging' and 'stealing'?

Looking closely

- After Tree-ear sees the rice pouring out from the man's backpack, his thoughts 'wrestled with one another'. Why did the writer choose the word 'wrestle'? (line 16)

- What is a 'temporary patch'? How does the man make it? (lines 34 and 35)

- Which words tell you that Tree-ear is respectful towards the man carrying the rice?

- Think of another adverb you could use instead of 'ruefully' (line 26).

Talking points

1 What lessons do you think Tree-ear learns from his experience?

2 What does Crane-man mean by 'Work gives a man dignity, stealing takes it away'? (line 47)

How do people try to help others?

Web advertisement

The Abandoned Street Kids of Brazil Trust (TASK) is an organization that runs a number of projects to help the many homeless children and young people who live on the streets of Rio de Janeiro in Brazil. The trust runs children's homes in the city for children they have rescued from the dangerous streets.

Another of their projects is Epsom College Farm, situated 90 miles from Rio de Janeiro, where there is a banana plantation, a citrus orchard and a vegetable garden. On this farm, boys from the children's homes in the city are taught farming skills. They produce vegetables, fruit, eggs and honey, which are sent back to the children's homes in Rio.

To raise money for their projects, the trust also offers *ecotours*, which it calls 'working holidays with a difference'.

> ### GLOSSARY
>
> An **ecotour** is 'an ecologically friendly tour'. 'Eco' is used as a prefix for many new words to do with the conservation of the environment. **W**
> The name of the country **Brazil** is spelt with a 'z' in English. The official language of Brazil is Portuguese, which spells *Brasil* with an 's'.

Map of Brazil in South America.

Talking points

1 Explain to a partner the work done by this trust. A 'trust' is another name for a charitable organization.

2 You have probably heard of an international charitable organization like the Red Cross. Do you know about a charitable organization which helps people in your country? What kind of work does it do?

3 How do you think the Chinese proverb at the beginning of this unit fits the work of TASK? ('Give me a fish and I eat for a day; teach me to fish and I eat for a lifetime.')

4 What do you know of the vegetation in Brazil? Point out the approximate location of the Amazon rainforest on the map on this page.

TASK BRASIL
The Abandoned Street Kids of Brazil Trust

Home | About | Task Brasil | Get Involved | Donations | News | Projects | Events | Shop | Our Supporters | Contact us

14–22 February: A Green Samba

Here in Rio de Janeiro we wait for the last of the heavy rains before planting our first vegetables. The period from the end of February until the beginning of March is the best time. For this first ecotour of the year, we will prepare the vegetable garden using organic methods. Garden beds damaged by the rains will be repaired and the soil improved.

The work will be rewarding and fulfilling and the boys living on the farm will join us in our daily activities and during our leisure time. At the end of the ecotour we will leave behind us a garden ready to produce healthy food for TASK Brasil's homes.

25 July – 1 August: The Banana Adventure

The taste of bananas will never be the same after you have taken part in our July ecotour! Banana trees only produce one bunch of bananas in their lifetime. Once the bunch is ready to be harvested, the tree is chopped down and the same roots produce another tree. TASK Brasil has opened its new home for 7- to 11-year-old children and plans to open a new house for teenage girls. We will need a lot more bananas!

Come to help us plant banana trees at Epsom College Farm and you will see the many smiling faces which you are helping. Planting will involve physical work, but we will make sure that you have plenty of time to relax. You can shower under the refreshing waterfalls of the rain forest, and enjoy the delicious traditional cuisine. An ecotour with TASK Brasil is a humanitarian experience that you will never forget.

www.taskbrazil.org.uk

Talking points

1 Does the writer make you think that an ecotour would be worthwhile?

2 If you went on an ecotour, what do you think you would enjoy most? Why?

3 Do you think there would be some parts of the ecotour you would not enjoy? Why?

4 Do you know which fruits and vegetables are grown in your own country and are most suitable to your climate zone?

Wordpool

organic

method

leisure

to relax

humanitarian

Writing David's diary

David, who is from London, went on one of the TASK ecotours, and the following is an extract from the diary he wrote describing his first two days.

Wordpool

jeep	manure
to sow	lethal
machete	blisters
barrow	

Toolkit

You will use the first-person singular and plural pronouns when you write a diary.

First-person pronouns include the speaker: 'I', 'we', 'us', 'our', 'my'.

Wednesday, February 16th

We arrived late last night in a jeep which bumped its way along rough, mud tracks. After a night's sleep and breakfast overlooking the beautiful forest we were ready for work. And what work! I can hardly lift my pen to write. All day long we've been clearing an area ready for planting and sowing. This involved cutting undergrowth with a machete, and carting away barrow loads of sand and earth. We think we work hard in the office, but this is real work.

Thursday, February 17th

Today we heaved bag after bag after bag of manure into the earth. I lost count of how many. We were warned against the little brown spiders on the forest floor, which are lethal. A bite would kill you so, despite the heat, we made sure our trousers were tucked into our boots. I slipped and fell in the mud over and over again, but we all laughed each time. I'm sure the muscles in my arms are bigger than they were yesterday but I have blisters on my hands. In the evening we were able to meet some of the boys at one of the hostels and it was great to know our work was really making a difference to their lives.

David's tour continued for another week, and included two rest days on a local beach. He kept a diary throughout to remind him of what he did and to reflect on what was being achieved.

- Imagine that you are David on the ecotour.
- Write diary entries for three more days from his tour.
- Use information from the web advertisement to give you further ideas for what to include, and make up additional activities yourself.

Make a list of as many words as you can that are connected with providing food for a family or a community. Do the word search below after you have read the poem on page 85.

Think of all the tasks which have to be done if you keep animals and chickens, grow crops, make flour and feed your family (all without any machines or gadgets to help you!).

C	Z	L	M	C	R	O	P	S	P
O	L	A	C	H	E	D	F	Q	U
O	S	B	D	I	G	G	I	N	G
K	E	O	F	C	W	E	E	D	R
A	W	U	R	K	B	C	L	M	A
H	A	R	V	E	S	T	D	P	Z
O	T	W	H	N	H	J	S	M	I
K	E	S	O	S	W	O	R	K	N
N	R	O	T	O	I	L	I	N	G

Poetry

Do you think it is possible to feed all the people on our planet? Where resources are scarce, providing food for even one family can be hard work. The following poem is about the life of an African woman from Malawi who works hard to provide for her family.

Word origins

The English word *thatch* comes from the Old Norse *thak*, meaning roof. It is generally used to refer to the straw or similar material used to provide roof cover.

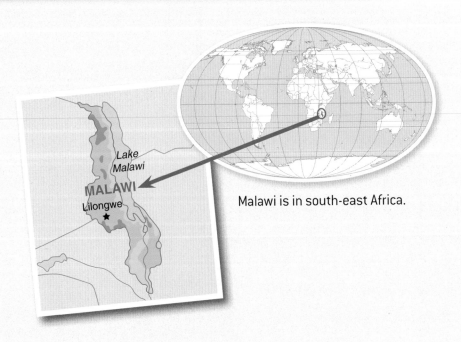

Malawi is in south-east Africa.

❧ Why the Old Woman Limps ❧

Do you know why the old woman sings?
She is sixty years old with six grandchildren to look after
While her sons and wives are gone south to dig gold.
Each day she milks the goat, sells the milk to buy soap,
5   Feeds and washes the children, and tethers the goat.
In the evening she tells them all stories of old at the
fireside:
I know why the old woman sings.

Do you know when the old woman sleeps?
10   She rests with the dark, at night she thinks of
Tomorrow: she's to feed the children and graze the goat.
She's to weed the garden, water the seedling beans,
The thatch has to be mended, the barnyard cleared.
Maize pounded, chaff winnowed, millet ground, fire lit …
15   I do not know when the old woman sleeps.

Do you know why the old woman limps?
She goes to fetch water in the morning
and the well is five miles away,
Goes to fetch firewood with her axe
20   and the forest is five miles the other way,
Goes to the fields to look for pumpkin leaves
leaving the goat tethered to the well tree
And hurries home to the children to cook:
I know why the old woman limps.

LUPENGA MPHANDE

Wordpool

to limp (title)
to tether (line 5)
to weed (12)
seedling (12)

Comprehension

1 Who is the woman looking after and providing food for?

2 What kind of work does she do? What kind of rest does she have?

3 Which of her tasks would you least like to do? Give your reasons.

4 For how long does the woman work each day?

5 How important is the goat to the woman and her family?

Looking closely

1 To whom do you think the questions in the poem are addressed?

2 What do the questions tell you about the old woman's life?

3 What are 'stories of old'? (line 6)

4 Write down synonyms for 'graze' and 'tethered'. (lines 11 and 22).

5 Explain in your own words where the woman's sons and their wives have gone.

6 Write down all the verbs which tell you what the old woman does in the day. What sort of actions do the verbs suggest?

Writing a poem

What does the woman have to do each day after she wakes up? What do you have to do? What do these tasks reveal about you?

- Make a list of the things you have to do each day after you wake up.
- Write your own poem starting with the words: 'Do you know why …'
  Start your final line with the words: 'I know why …'
  (Your poem does not have to rhyme!) W

Extension reading

From *Tales from China* by Cyril Birch

This Chinese fairytale offers further insights into how eating and preparing food is central to our desire for a happy home life. It tells the story of Hsieh Tuan and his struggles to find a wife who can cook and keep house for him.

✂ **The Dinner that Cooked Itself** ✂

Of all the quests a young man must follow, none is more difficult than the quest for the girl who will marry him, be his wife and live with him happily ever after. And in China in the old times, he would have many an obstacle to overcome
5 before his search ended. So it was that Hsieh Tuan failed time and again to find himself a bride.

Tuan was a tall, handsome youth of 18. He was only a humble clerk in the magistrate's court, but he worked always with a will, and his honesty and respectful bearing impressed all
10 who knew him. His father and mother had both died when he was very small, but a kind neighbour, old Wang, had taken him in and treated him as one of his own sons. Now that Tuan had reached manhood he moved into a little house of his own. Not far from the house he had a small strip of land,
15 where he tended his rice-plants and beans each day when his duties at court were done.

It was old Wang who hired a go-between to seek out a wife for Tuan. The go-between suggested Miss Ch'en, the pretty daughter of a farmer on the outskirts of the town.

20 But when the dates of birth were compared, it was found that Miss Ch'en had been born in the year of the cat. Now Tuan belonged to the year of the dog; and with cat and dog under one roof there would never be a day's peace in the house. The go-between tried again a little further away. But
25 the problem this time was the characters with which the young lady wrote her name. They contained a sign which

Wordpool

quest (line 1)

obstacle (4)

humble (7)

magistrate (8)

to cultivate (36)

rarity (49)

to squat (66)

appealing (75)

to ply (77)

jade (119)

meant 'wood', and Tuan's name contained 'earth'. Now wood overcomes earth, as a wooden plough turns a furrow, so that married to this girl Tuan would never have been master in his 30 own house.

One match after another was considered and rejected. Even when everything else was right, people would object that Tuan was too poor to marry their daughter. But none of this made any difference to Tuan's daily work, which began at cock-crow 35 when he left for the magistrate's court, and ended at nightfall when he returned from cultivating his tiny field.

One night Tuan, his hoe over his shoulder, was making his way slowly along the narrow path which joined his field to his house. He had worked even later than usual, and at dark sat down on 40 a dyke and waited for the moon to rise. The moon was full, and its light now lay like snow on the thatch of his own cottage and sparkled like frost on the tiled roofs of his wealthier neighbours. He looked down to follow the winding of the narrow path. The moonlight glimmered on a stone by the edge of the path at his 45 feet. But the stone had never been there before. And was it really a stone after all? It was rounded, and pointed at the top. He bent down for a closer look. Not a stone, but a snail – an enormous, giant snail, quite the size of a small bucket.

Of course, it was a sign of great good luck to find such a rarity.
50 Delighted, Tuan raised the snail gently in his hands and hurried
on home. On the way he picked some succulent leaves for it to
eat, and these he put together with the snail in a large, roomy
earthenware storage-jar which stood just inside his door. He
went to bed still rejoicing over his good fortune. In the morning
55 when he woke, his first thought was to look inside the jar, and
he was pleased to see that the snail had eaten a hearty
breakfast.

And now a very curious thing happened. Tuan went off to the
court as usual and came back home in the afternoon to have a
60 bite to eat before going out to his field. But when he entered his
little house he found the table set with bowl and chopsticks.
Steam rose temptingly from a dish of cooked rice and vegetables,
and on the newly swept floor was his large washing-bowl, filled
with hot water ready for him to use!

65 'How kind people are,' Tuan thought as he washed his hands
and face and squatted down to attack his dinner. 'It must be
Mrs Wang who has stolen in here secretly to give me such a
pleasant surprise. What a thoughtful thing to do!'

Never in his life had he tasted such delicious cooking. As soon
70 as he had washed up he hurried to Mrs Wang's house to thank
her. But he was mistaken. Mrs Wang had not been near his
cottage, and could not imagine who it might have been.

Yet when he returned from the court again the following day,
exactly the same thing had happened again. Tuan was greeted
75 as he entered the house by an even more appealing smell from
the table, where a dish of little fried balls of pork lay beside the
steaming rice. While he hungrily plied his chopsticks, Tuan tried
hard to decide who it might be. At last he hit on an idea – it was
the pretty Miss Ch'en, who could not be his wife because she
80 was born in the wrong year, but had taken pity on his loneliness
and decided to help him until he should have a wife of his
own.

So round he went to the farm on the outskirts of the town, to thank Miss Ch'en for her kindness. But Miss Ch'en seemed to
85 know no more about it than Mrs Wang had done. When he pleaded with her to tell him the truth, she began to tease him, 'I don't believe your story at all. I think you really have a wife already but are keeping her secret. She is in your house all the time, but you won't let anyone see her and are pretending it is
90 someone else who is cooking your meals for you!'

Tuan returned home more mystified than ever. On his way he picked some fresh shoots of bamboo to feed his snail, which still seemed very happy to roam about inside its huge earthenware jar.

95 Every day for over a week the same thing went on happening. Each day Tuan would come home to find his room swept, his washing-water all heated and ready and his dinner waiting on the table. The news spread among all the neighbours, but no one offered to explain the mystery. At last Tuan determined to
100 get to the bottom of it. He left his house as usual at the first crow of the cock. But as soon as the sun was up he came secretly back, and hid outside the fence to watch what might happen in the house.

For a while all was still. Then, suddenly, there was a movement:
105 through the doorway he saw a hand appear out of the huge earthenware jar. After the hand another hand; and a lovely young girl, beautifully dressed in a silk robe, climbed out of the jar and crossed the room to the stove in the corner.

Quickly Tuan left his hiding-place and entered the house. His
110 first concern was to look inside the jar – no snail was there, but only an empty shell! In the corner by the stove the girl pressed herself against the wall in alarm.

'Who are you?' asked Tuan. 'Where do you come from, and why are you looking after my house for me?'

115 The girl said nothing. Her frightened glance darted about the room, and she tried to dash across to the earthenware jar, but Tuan prevented her.

Finally she spoke. Her voice was clear and sweet like a tinkling of jades. 'I am a fairy,' she said, 'and my name is White Wave.
120 The Lord of Heaven took pity on you because you are an orphan and live alone. And because you work hard and are honest and polite, he sent me to look after you. I was to stay with you for ten years, until you grew rich and married a wife. Then I was to leave you and return to Fairyland. But now you have spied
125 on me in secret, and you have seen my true form. This is not permitted to a mortal. I must leave you at once. You must continue to work hard at court and cultivate your land with all your strength. But you may keep the shell which I left in the jar. Use it for storing rice, and empty it only when hunger threatens.
130 You will find that it will at once fill up again.'

In vain Tuan pleaded with her to stay. No effort would succeed; she had to go. The sky darkened and a storm blew up, the wind howled, and rain lashed the roof. White Wave ran lightly across the room and out of the door, spread her arms wide and soared
135 away, borne by the raging wind. As suddenly as it had started the storm came to an end, and Tuan was left in the calm morning, his eyes filled with tears.

Hsieh Tuan built a little shrine to the fairy White Wave, and he did not fail to sacrifice there on feast days. From that time
140 onwards he was never short of food. And although he never became outstandingly wealthy, he married a wife who at last made him very happy all his life. Nor did he always remain a humble clerk, but ended up by becoming a district magistrate himself.

CYRIL BIRCH

Comprehension

1 Why can't anyone find Tuan a wife? What obstacles are there?

2 Why do you think people use go-betweens? What is their purpose?

3 Who is the snail, and why does she visit Tuan? Why does she leave?

4 How does the shell continue to be of help to Tuan?

6 Wildlife

How do humans and animals live together?

In this unit you will:

Experience
- Ancient Rome
- Botswana
- Greece
- Siberia, Russia
- India

Read
- prose non-fiction
- a comic strip
- prose fiction
- a letter to the editor
- a true story

Create
- a dialogue
- a comic strip
- a journal entry
- a letter of reply
- a story

Everywhere the People of the Sea told him the same things. Seals had come to these islands once upon a time, but men had killed them all off.

From 'The White Seal' in *The Jungle Book* by Rudyard Kipling, 1894

Have you ever visited the Colosseum in Rome? It is the remains of a gigantic stadium in the capital of the Roman Empire, that two thousand years ago could hold 50,000 people. Today, an audience would be there to watch a football match or a pop concert. Do you know what the people crowded in to see two thousand years ago in Rome?

The remains of the Colosseum in Rome.

The performances in the Colosseum started in 80 CE. In these performances, skilled fighting men called gladiators fought each other, and also fought wild animals. Lions, bears, panthers and leopards were just some of the animals captured for these popular contests that went on for hundreds of years, and may have had an impact on animal populations.

When animal populations decrease year by year, they eventually become endangered. This means they are in danger of completely dying out and becoming extinct. Both their habitats, the places where they live and feed, and the animals themselves have to be protected.

The relationship between humans and animals is complicated. Many people love to see animals living in their natural habitat, and are concerned about the effects of human activity, but human beings can also place themselves at risk when they encounter wild animals.

A Roman mosaic of gladiators and a tiger.

Talking points

1 What wild animals have you seen?
2 Do you know of any animals, birds or sea creatures anywhere in the world which are now endangered?
3 Can you think of ways in which people could protect animals?

Prose non-fiction

From *Whatever You Do, Don't Run* by Peter Allison

The following is a personal account of an adventure in an African wildlife park in the Okavango Delta. This is an area of wetland in the middle of the Kalahari Desert in Botswana. Tourists 'go on safari' there. This means that they go with a guide on foot, in a vehicle, or in a boat, to see the animals and birds which are protected from hunters and poachers. The writer is a guide in the wildlife park.

The guide is approaching the end of a safari walk with his group when an unexpected event puts his skills to the test.

ಉಾ **Wild Buffalo** ☙

At the edge of the plain, a group of zebra was slowly making its way to the shade of the trees. Apart from the zebra, nothing moved as I led my group of tourists forward. They were happy now that the camp was near and they would
5 soon have a cool drink. When we were half way across the plain, I caught a glimpse of a bush some distance away which was shaking. As there was no breeze, I knew an animal must be causing the disturbance. I raised my hand, motioning to the group to stay silent.

10 A buffalo emerged from the bush he had wrecked, obviously in a dangerous mood. With no breeze, he wouldn't smell us, but he'd soon see us. I made slow hand signs, directing the group to squat whilst I kept my eyes on the buffalo. He hadn't spotted us. Then I heard a sound.

15 'Click, whirr, click, whirr.'

I turned round quickly and my eyes confirmed my fears. Jacques, a young member of the group, was standing up taking photos, and the buffalo was now glaring at this new object with his yellow-ringed eyes. The huge animal stepped
20 forward, horns high and nose glistening. I had to make a plan, and make it fast. I looked at the flat plain. We would never make it to the trees, but there was a large termite

GLOSSARY

The phrase **to take the bait** is often used as a metaphor. A fisherman puts a worm on the end of his fishing line to encourage the fish to bite, and so be caught. Hunters may put a piece of meat inside a trap to catch a wild animal. The worm and the meat are bait. Can you work out why the safari guide uses this expression?

Wordpool

Discuss the meaning of the following words taken from the extract.

plain (line 1)

to squat (13)

mound (23)

grove (29)

to graze (30)

to huddle (34)

Make your own wordpool of any other unfamiliar words and phrases you come across.

mound not far away. I waved for the group to follow me to it and whispered for them to wait for me there. The
25 buffalo was slowly moving forward.

I started to run across the plain back to where we had come from. Glancing over my shoulder, I saw that the buffalo had taken the bait and was watching me with his nostrils flaring and his head held high. Having reached the grove of trees,
30 I crept silently towards the group of grazing zebra. Suddenly I burst out of my cover, waving my arms and shouting. The zebras ran away, and as they ran, they made a whistling noise which warned other animals of danger. The buffalo, now close to the termite mound where the tourists huddled,
35 heard the zebras' warning whistle. He knew that whatever was pursuing the zebra was a danger to him, too. In an instant, he changed course and ran off in a cloud of dust behind the zebras.

I ran back to the termite mound and collected my frightened
40 group. As we walked back to the camp no one spoke a word to Jacques.

PETER ALLISON

Comprehension

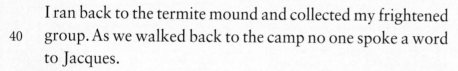

1 Why is it obvious that the buffalo is in a dangerous mood?

2 What does Jacques do to attract the buffalo's attention?

3 What is the guide's plan to save his group from being approached by the buffalo?

4 Why does the zebras' whistling make the buffalo run?

5 What does Jacques not understand about wild animals?

6 How is Jacques treated as the group walk back to the camp?

7 What might have happened if the guide hadn't been able to make the buffalo run away?

Writing a dialogue

Write a short dialogue between the guide and Jacques reflecting one part of the event above, or a conversation after the event. Perhaps the guide explains to Jacques why everyone is annoyed with him. Write the dialogue like an extract from a play. Punctuate your dialogue like the sample provided. When writing a dialogue, you do not use quotation marks as you do when you are writing direct speech.

Safari guide: I'd like to speak to you, Jacques.

Jacques: Sure. Is it about what happened?

Why is it important to learn about animals?

A comic strip

Here is a comic strip that aims to teach people something about wild animals. This strip focuses on their sense of vision. What does the eye position tell you about an animal?

Wordpool

keen (frame 1)

amphibians (5)

turret (5)

protruding (5)

scout (5)

Making a comic strip

Make your own comic strip about wild animals. You will need to research a particular animal or aspect of animals, such as their sense of smell. Then set out the information with illustrations. You can create your own illustrations on paper, or you can cut and paste printed images from magazines and leaflets. Alternatively, you could work on a computer screen, using images you find on the Internet. Whichever method you use, make sure your work looks attractive and interesting. **W**

Here are some suggestions for research topics:

- types of fur or skin for protection
- cold-blooded or warm-blooded creatures
- types of wings
- types of habitats
- animals in extreme climates.

Look at these pictures to add to your list of topics

Prose fiction

From *Watching* by Judy Allen

In the following text, Jenny is on holiday in Greece with her parents and older brother, Joe. They want to visit a tiny rocky island, visible from the mainland, but have trouble finding a boat to take them. They finally persuade one young fisherman, Stefanos, to take them there in his boat. As the family swim and picnic, Jenny explores the island and is very excited when she sees a seal dive into a cave beneath the rocks.

❧ Jenny's Secret ❧

I wondered if the cave would have a hole in its roof. And it did. I searched around and I found the opening, half hidden by a little bush. At first when I looked in all I could see was a pattern of shimmering green and gold all over the cave
5 walls. Then I could make out a big cavern with a stony floor and rock shelves. And I was there, looking in, when the seal swam in through the opening and hauled himself out of the water and onto the little beach inside the cave. It was only then that I noticed three more seals lying on rock shelves
10 high up.

Two of them had babies. I could hear the little bleating noise from the pups. It was the most magical and beautiful thing I'd ever heard. I realised that for once in my life I knew something that not one of the rest of my family knew. I stood
15 up, and saw that Stefanos was bringing his boat in closer. He was waving at us and shouting that there was a storm coming and we must return. Suddenly clouds came over the sun and I could feel the wind getting stronger. Stefanos kept the boat steady and he and I waited for the others to join us.
20 It was then that he said that he knew what I'd found. He told me it was the last hiding place of that seal family and that if they were disturbed the mothers might abandon their pups, or even kill them. That was why he tried to stop people going there.

25 'I didn't disturb them!' I cried.

Wordpool

shimmering [line 4]

to haul [7]

bleating [11]

'No, I'm sure you didn't,' said Stefanos. 'But will you betray them?'

He glanced at my parents and Joe packing up on the beach.

30 'My family wouldn't hurt them.'

'But they would want to look, wouldn't they? They would dive down, just once, thinking there could be no harm in that. And later others might hear them talking about what they had seen and come out to see for themselves.'

35 I watched my family wading slowly towards us. I wanted to tell them about what I had seen so much that it almost hurt. Stefanos understood.

'I'll give you something else to tell them instead,' he said. 'Hundreds of years ago, people believed that a tent made of
40 sealskin would protect them from lightning.' The sky was dark and rain was starting. 'Will you tell them that and keep the seals' secret? For the seals' sake?'

And then everyone was climbing on board. The water was choppy and the weather was worsening.

45 'Someone doesn't mind the weather!' said my father suddenly.

There he was, my seal, his head just above the surface of the water.

'You'd think there would be a whole family of them, wouldn't
50 you?' said my mother.

It was almost unbearable. I said, 'I can tell you something none of you know.'

And I told them about the sealskin tent and lightning. I had kept the seals' secret. It was worth it for the seals – and for
55 the smile Stefanos gave me.

JUDY ALLEN

Comprehension

1 What is special about the place Jenny finds?

2 What would happen if people came to look at the seals?

3 Why might telling her family about the seals be bad for the seals, even though her family would never want to hurt them?

4 What is the significance of the story about the sealskin?

Looking closely

1 Which verb means to leave behind, or to desert? (paragraph 2)

2 What does 'betray' mean? What would happen to the seals if Jenny 'betrayed' them? (line 26)

3 What kind of movement is 'wading' ? (line 35)

4 Which adjective towards the end of the text tells you that the water is beginning to get rough?

5 Which word in the text with a prefix of un- or in- means the same as 'intolerable'?

Talking points

1 What is the best holiday you have ever had?
2 Tell the rest of your group about your holiday.
3 Invite your listeners to ask you questions.

Journal

Using all the ideas from the holiday stories you have exchanged with your group, write a journal entry about a memorable experience.

Toolkit

Many of the extracts in this unit use an 's' to show belonging (the possessive).

These include: 'the zebra's warning whistle' (singular); 'the seals' secret' (plural, with an apostrophe after the 's').

List other examples you can find in this unit, and identify if they are singular or plural.

Why is it difficult to protect animals?

Sometimes the interests of human beings and of the animals who live in the same area may be in conflict. There may be good reasons why it is difficult to protect the local wildlife.

Saving the Siberian tiger

Around Vladivostok are uninhabited forests known as *taiga*. For many centuries, the forests have provided a habitat for Siberian tigers where they can live and feed undisturbed by human beings. However, Siberian tigers are now endangered, which means they may become extinct.

The letters page of a magazine or newspaper prints letters sent in by readers to express their thoughts or opinions. Sometimes a reader's letter ends by asking a question, in the hope that someone else will write to supply the answer.

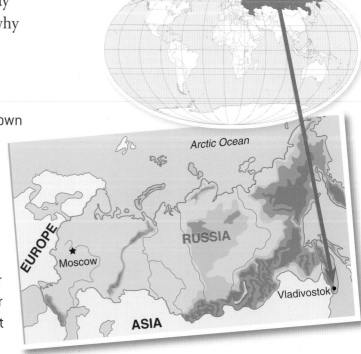

GLOSSARY

The Russian word **taiga** (тайга) is pronounced the same as 'tiger' in English but has a very different meaning. It is the name given to the vast areas of forest in Siberia in the Russian Far East.

Wordpool

to poach (paragraph 2)

illegal (2)

boar (2)

logging (3)

 # Letter to the editor

Recently I travelled to Vladivostok, where the beautiful Siberian tigers live in the nearby forests. I joined a group tour to see the animals in their natural habitat. I was shocked to learn that since the 1990s the habitat of the Siberian tigers has been taken over more and more by human beings.

Unemployment is high in the area and many people have turned to poaching and hunting. These activities are illegal. They are killing animals such as the wild boar and deer, which the tigers feed on. Some people are even killing the tigers. A tiger's skin can be sold for as much money as a year's income, and the bones and internal organs are valuable for Chinese medicine. Although patrols have reduced the number of killings, tigers are still dying.

Life is harsh for the local people, and forests are a good source of income for them; they cut down the trees and transport the logs for sale, sometimes legally and sometimes illegally. But this logging is destroying the tigers' habitat. Both the tigers and the people are struggling to survive.

I have heard that the government is trying to solve the conflicts between humans and animals. But there are only about 350 adult tigers left! I'm wondering what is being done, and if any international organizations are trying to save these amazing creatures?

Sabine Ketelsen, Hamburg

1 With a partner, list the human activities mentioned in the letter which have had an impact on the Siberian tiger population.

2 Think of at least two things that could be done to help solve the conflicts between humans and animals.

Toolkit

The two words *affect* (verb) and *effect* (verb and noun) are frequently confused in English.

- 'To affect' (verb) means to have an impact.
  Example: The human population has *affected* wildlife habitats.

- An 'effect' (noun) is the result or impact of something.
  Example: The *effect* was a further decline in the population of the tigers.

- 'To effect' (verb) is to bring something about.
  Example: To effect an increase in the tiger population, illegal poaching must stop.

Make a list of further examples from this unit. **W**

Toolkit

A *prefix* is a group of letters (or a single letter) attached to the beginning of a word, which changes its meaning.

There are many pairs of words in English where a prefix is added to the start of a word to form its opposite. An example from the letter on page 101 is 'legally'/ 'illegally'. How many more pairs can you think of? **W**

Writing a letter

Write a letter in reply to Sabine Ketelsen. Find out which organizations are trying to help save the Siberian tiger, and explain three or four of the things they are doing. Begin your letter with 'Dear Ms Ketelsen'.

What happens when animals are a threat?

Sometimes it is difficult for wild animals to be protected because they pose a serious danger to people or to their domestic animals. This is a situation that needs careful management.

Prose non-fiction

The events described in the following story happened in northern India in the 1930s. At that time, tigers regularly killed the cattle belonging to people living in isolated villages, and it was not unusual for people to be attacked. Tigers have been known to enter houses and drag sleeping villagers from their beds. Although most tigers do not kill human beings, once a tiger has killed a person, they are more likely to do so again.

ೞ The Man-eating Tiger ೲ

Vikram was an old man. As a young man, he had been a soldier and he wanted his only son to have a career in the army. So, just after his eighteenth birthday, Vikram's son Dileep travelled to the town, some distance away. He was
5 accepted into the army and given two days' leave before starting his training.

When Dileep arrived back in the village, a crowd of villagers welcomed him. They told him that his father was working on his land at the farthest end of the village and would not
10 be back before nightfall. So, after lunch with his neighbours, a party of about 20 young men set off to gather leaves for cattle fodder. For several months the villagers had gathered leaves only from nearby trees, because two women collecting grass had been killed by a tiger in the surrounding forest.
15 But now there were not enough leaves to feed the cattle, and the men had to go into the forest again. They walked beyond

Wordpool

nightfall (line 10)

fodder (12)

cultivated (17)

lantern (39)

to glint (46)

the cultivated fields, up the valley and into the dense forest.

Here the men separated, each one climbing a tree and cutting
20 the thin branches. They then tied them into bundles and
returned as quickly as they could to the village. Each man
sang as he walked to keep up his courage. From among the
trees, the man-eating tiger heard the men's voices. Silently,
he left his cover and followed a cattle track across the
25 stream.

Dileep was high in a bauhinia tree, the upper branches of
which leaned over a small ravine. The tiger saw Dileep and
hid himself behind a fallen tree some distance away. Dileep
finished cutting the leaves and started to bundle them up.
30 He noticed that two of the branches which he had cut had
fallen into the ravine. He jumped down to collect them. As
he bent to pick up the branches, the tiger leaped on him and
killed him.

Vikram returned to the village at sunset and was delighted
35 to hear that his son had been accepted in the army. But why
had Dileep not returned from gathering fodder? Vikram shut
up his cattle safely for the night, and still his son had not
returned. Darkness was falling and the villagers were inside
their houses for the night. Vikram took a lantern and went
40 out to look for Dileep.

Like all the villagers, Vikram believed evil spirits roamed in
the forest at night, and he knew that a man-eating tiger had
killed there. Nevertheless, he spent the entire night crossing
and re-crossing the forest as he searched for his son. As the
45 sun rose the next day, Vikram was resting on a rock above
the ravine when he saw blood glinting on a nearby stone.
He knew then, even before he found Dileep's body, that his
son was dead.

Not long afterwards, the man-eating tiger was hunted and
50 shot. Vikram was satisfied.

GLOSSARY

A **bauhinia** tree is a beautiful flowering tree, also known as the orchid tree, which grows in tropical countries.

A **ravine** is a narrow valley or gorge with steep sides.

104

Comprehension

1 Where was Vikram when his son came home from the town?

2 Why hadn't the villagers been to the forest to gather leaves in recent months?

3 Why did the villagers have to go to the forest that day?

4 What mistake did Dileep make when gathering the leaves, which resulted in his death?

5 What dangers did Vikram face as he searched through the night for his son?

Talking points

1 What have you learned about the character of Vikram from this story? Do you think he was brave? Why was he satisfied when he heard that the tiger had been killed?

2 Do you think the tiger should have been shot? Can you think of any other solution to the villagers' problem?

Writing a story

You have read several stories in this unit. Now it's your turn to write a story involving an animal. Your story may be true or imaginary. You may like to write about your pet, or a wild animal.

- Identify some features you have enjoyed in the stories you have read.
- Think of an idea for a good plot for an animal story, perhaps involving someone in danger, or a conflict between humans and animals.
- Plan your story carefully, including precise details about the setting and the human and animal characters. Describe the nature of the relationship and the dilemmas they face. Include a dramatic scene at either the beginning or the end of the story. **W**

Living together

How do we manage scarce resources?

In this unit you will:

Experience
- the Netherlands and Dubai
- Ethiopia
- Robinson Crusoe's island

Read
- factual text
- a folk tale
- poetry
- classic fiction
- a short story

Create
- direct speech
- a presentation
- a folk tale
- a poem
- journal entries

The perpetual struggle for room and food ...

Thomas Malthus, *Essay on the Principle of Population*, 1798

Talking points

1 By how much has the population in your country increased in the past 200 years?

2 What problems are caused by an increase in the population?

Some experts now think that by 2030 there will be 8.3 billion people on planet Earth. There are many problems caused by this growing population. Our Earth has a great many valuable resources, such as water, minerals, and fertile land. How do we make sure there is enough to go around?

Writing and punctuating speech

Look at the pictures that follow.

- Talk about the lives of the people shown in each picture.
- Imagine what the characters may be thinking and feeling.
- Fill in the speech bubbles with appropriate comments.
- Write out what each person is saying, using direct speech.

Toolkit

When you punctuate *direct speech*, you need to show who is speaking, and what they are saying. It also helps to use descriptive words that reflect the attitude of the speaker.

Example: 'I'm going to be late again,' sighed the businessman.

Noisy aircraft fly low over houses near the airport.

Golf courses for tourists take water away from the local people who need it.

Over-fishing has reduced the number of fish in the sea.

The land is over-grazed and there is no longer enough food for the community's animals.

Many commuters driving to work each day join one big traffic jam.

Can we create more land?

1 Before you read the following text, discuss with your group what you know about the Netherlands.

2 Can you find the Netherlands on a map?

3 What sort of natural features do you find in the Netherlands?

4 Look at the two maps of the Netherlands. Can you see how much of the land has been reclaimed from the sea?

Wordpool

Discuss the meaning of the following words:

to reclaim

densely

artificial

to expand

expensive

environmentalist

oppose

Make your own wordpool of any other unfamiliar words you come across.

The Netherlands means 'the low-lying lands', and it is one of the world's most densely populated countries. There are 485 people per square kilometre, and one quarter of the country is below sea level.

There is an old saying in the Netherlands: 'God made the world, but the Dutch made the Netherlands.' The Dutch have been reclaiming land from the sea for centuries. In fact, a thousand years ago 60 per cent of the Netherlands was under water.

Word origins

Nether is an old English word, meaning 'low'. It gives the Netherlands and the lower part of the River Rhine that flows through Germany its name: *Neder Rijn* in Dutch.

The parts of the Netherlands, in north-western Europe, which are above sea level.

The Netherlands, showing reclaimed land (areas in white).

Artificial islands in Dubai and the Netherlands

This is Palm Jumeirah Island in Dubai. It is a man-made island built for tourists in the shallow waters of the Arabian Gulf, where the waves are no more than two metres high.

Designed by a Dutch construction company with experience in land reclamation, it has also inspired the design of a new island off the coast of the Netherlands.

The plan is for an island 50 kilometres long that will provide extra land for housing and farming. 'We are hungry for land,' says a Dutch politician. 'We need a huge area for building.' As in other countries, the population of the Netherlands is expanding.

If it is built, this island will be in the stormy North Sea, where waves can be ten metres high. Scientists agree that sea levels are likely to rise in the future. This means that the island would have to be built high above sea level, which would be very expensive.

Environmentalists oppose the plan. Building the island would require hundreds of millions of tonnes of sand and sea to be moved. They are worried about the effect this would have on the marine life in the area. The real effects of building the island will be known only after it has been built.

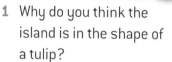

Looking closely

1 Why do you think the island is in the shape of a tulip?

2 Do you think islands should be created? With a partner, make a list of reasons for and against building artificial islands.

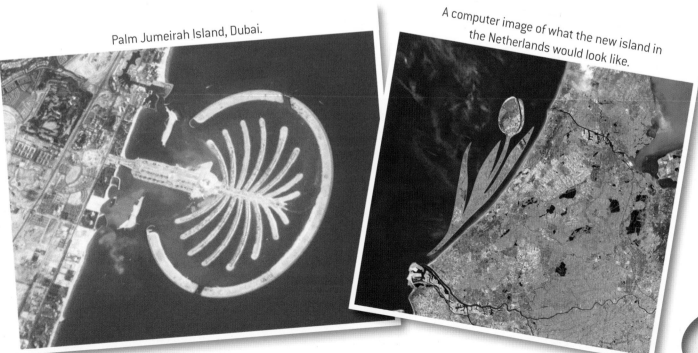

Palm Jumeirah Island, Dubai.

A computer image of what the new island in the Netherlands would look like.

Presenting your design for an island

Imagine that you have been asked to enter a competition to design a new island. You are one of ten designers and at the end of the competition, one design will be chosen.

When you draw an image of your island, will you look at digital maps on the internet, photographs of real islands, or some of the fantastic images from the early days of exploration? Think about the people who will settle there, and what kind of life they will lead.

- Create a drawing of your proposed island and give it a name.
- Decide where in the world this island should be.
- What would your island be used for?
- Write a short presentation, arguing the case for why your island should be built.

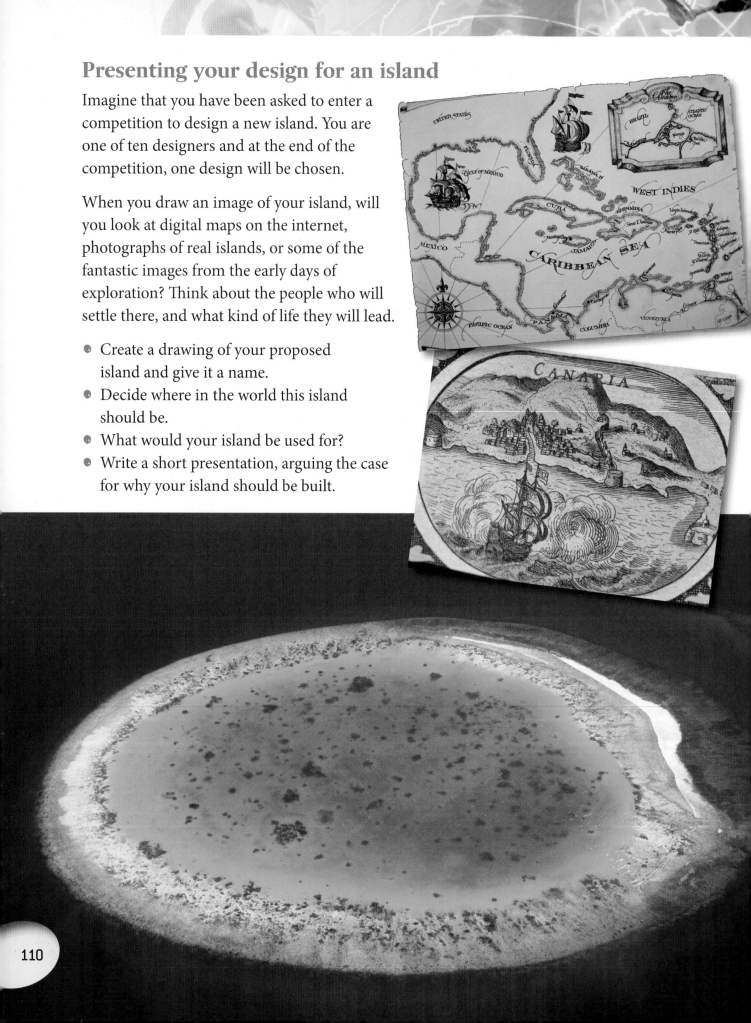

How do we share resources fairly?

A folk tale

Problems can be overcome by dividing resources more equally. The following text is a folk tale from Ethiopia. It is about two brothers whose rich old father died, and left all his wealth and land to his proud and selfish elder son. His younger son, who was kind and goodhearted, only received a rooster with fine red feathers.

‷The Red Rooster ‷

Harvest time came, and the elder brother gathered in his crops and filled his grain stores until they were overflowing, but he never gave any grain to the younger man.

‘It can't be helped,’ the younger brother said to his wife. ‘No
5   doubt he needs all the grain for himself.’

The rich brother sometimes killed a cow and gave feasts for his friends, but he never invited his brother.

‘Ah well,’ the younger brother said. ‘He is still my brother, after all.’ Then, one day, the elder brother fell ill. He sent for
10   the medicine man who came to examine him.

‘You won't get better,’ the medicine man said, ‘unless you eat the flesh of a big rooster with fine red feathers.’

‘I haven't got a rooster,’ the sick man cried.

‘No, but your brother has,’ said his wife. ‘That horrid thing!
15   It wakes me up every morning with its ugly crowing.’

‘Then go and ask my brother to give it to me,’ the older brother moaned. ‘And hurry up. I feel so ill I'm sure I'm about to die.’

His wife ran to the younger brother's house.

20   ‘Your elder brother's ill,’ she said. ‘And the only thing that can cure him is the flesh of a big rooster with fine red feathers.’

Wordpool

harvest (line 1)

to overflow (2)

horrid (14)

to slaughter (30)

to curse (48)

affectionately (54)

'Husband,' said the younger brother's wife. 'That rooster is the only thing we have.'

25 Her husband frowned at her.

'If my brother needs it, he must have it,' he said.

So he gave the rooster to his brother's wife, and she took it away and killed it and gave its meat to the sick man to eat.

Very soon the elder brother began to feel better.

30 'Slaughter a cow,' he said to his wife. 'Make a feast. Invite my friends. Let's celebrate my recovery.'

But he didn't invite his brother.

The feast was at its height and everyone was sitting at their ease, enjoying the tasty stews, when the elder brother felt

35 that something strange was happening to him. He touched his legs and felt his arms.

'Help!' he shouted. 'What's happening to me? I'm growing feathers!'

His wife and all his guests jumped up in horror. It was true.
40 Bright red feathers were growing all over the body of their host. The medicine man and the elders came running as soon as they heard the news. They sat down together to discuss the problem.

'You've been greedy,' they said at last to the sick man. 'You
45 took everything that your father left you and gave nothing to your brother. You even took his rooster, his only possession, without a word of thanks, although he gave it to you freely and generously. You will be cursed and your feathers will grow until he has forgiven you.'

50 At once the elder brother went to the younger brother and begged his forgiveness.

'Brother, forgive me,' he said. 'I've been selfish and greedy, and I took all you had without a word of thanks.'

His younger brother embraced him affectionately.

55 'Of course I forgive you,' he said, 'for we are brothers, after all.' At once the feathers dropped off the elder brother and he had a man's skin again. He shared his property equally with his younger brother, and from that time on they lived in harmony with each other.

Writing a folk tale

Folk tales, like the one that you have just read, are often simply written and constructed. They are usually designed to illustrate some kind of message, and present a story with a moral or lesson. In addition, they usually reflect the culture and traditions of the area they come from.

- Write your own folk tale. It can relate to a story you know, or make it up entirely.
- Base your story around a message about the way people behave, or the conflicts they face.
- Use a simple, clear style, and use paragraphs to structure your story. **W**

Comprehension

1 Who are the winners and who are the losers in this folk tale, and why?

2 What lessons do you think this folk tale teaches?

3 How would you have divided up the property left to the two brothers?

Poetry

Countries can be greedy as well as individuals. Which countries do you think use up most of the Earth's resources, and which use the least?

John Agard was born in Guyana and came to Britain as an adult in 1977. He was thinking about questions like this when he wrote the poem below.

❧ I'd like to squeeze ❧

I'd like to squeeze this round world
    into a new shape

    I'd like to squeeze this round world
        like a tube of toothpaste

        I'd like to squeeze this round world
          fair and square

          I'd like to squeeze it and squeeze it
            till everybody had an equal share

JOHN AGARD

Looking closely

1. Explain how John Agard thinks that 'squeezing' would help the world.

2. 'Like a tube of toothpaste' is a simile. How many more similes can you think of which would fit this line?

3. There is no punctuation in this poem. Why do you think the poet chose to use none?

4. Which words are repeated in the poem? What effect does the repetition have?

Toolkit

John Agard has set out his lines in a special way to *structure* his poem and emphasize the occasional rhyme.

- Look at how the rhyming of 'square' and 'share' is emphasized.

- Notice how Agard's poem appears to be moving across the page, to give the poem a sense of direction.

- Experiment with the layout of lines in your own poems.

Writing a poem

John Agard's poem is a simple one, with a clear message about the world. He uses the theme of shapes to illustrate his ideas, and crafts his poem using repetition and some rhyme.

- Write your own poem about the world's limited resources, in the style of Agard's poem.
- Choose an image to develop in your poem. W

Classic fiction

From *Robinson Crusoe* by Daniel Defoe

Robinson Crusoe is a novel by Daniel Defoe that was published nearly 300 years ago in 1719.

After he was shipwrecked on a tropical island, Crusoe managed to survive with only a few objects saved from the ship, including a gun and a packet of barley seeds. This short extract is about his struggle to produce the first crop in his new island home.

❧ My First Harvest ☙

The ground I had dug up for my crop of barley was not large, for I only had a small amount of seed. My hopes of gathering seed from my first crop had been destroyed. I had planted my first crop in the dry season and it had failed. I was pleased
5   to see my new crop growing well, but then I saw that I was in danger of losing it. Wild goats were devouring it. They were eating the green shoots as soon as they pushed through the earth.

With a great deal of hard work I made a hedge to fence in
10   my crop and tied my dog to the little gate which I also made. He barked all night long, the wild goats kept away and my barley grew strong and green. As it began to ripen and form ears of seed, my hopes of being able to make bread also grew.

15   But then my crop was under threat of ruin once more when I found flocks of fowl pecking at the seeds. I immediately shot at them, for I always had my gun with me, but more birds returned. I realized that they would destroy all my hopes and I would starve. I examined the damage and found
20   that if I could save what was left of my crop all was not lost.

I killed three of the birds and hung their bodies from the trees. The effect was marvellous. So long as my scarecrows

Wordpool

barley (line 1)

to devour (6)

fowl (16)

marvellous (23)

scarecrows (23)

25 hung there, the fowls came neither to my crops again, nor even to my part of the island. This I was very glad of, and at about the end of December, I harvested my crop. I was very relieved, and I now believed I would be able to supply myself with bread.

DANIEL DEFOE

Comprehension

1 In each of the first three paragraphs, Crusoe talks about his 'hopes'. Explain what his hopes are.

2 How does Crusoe overcome each of the problems he faces?

3 What does Crusoe mean when he says his crop is 'under threat of ruin'? (line 15)

Toolkit

Look at the way *there* and *their* are used in paragraph 4. These words are pronounced the same, but are spelled differently and have different meanings. Explain the meanings of *there* and *their* in this text. W

Journal

Robinson Crusoe had to defend his crop of barley from the wild goats and the birds. Write your account in the form of a journal written from a bird's point of view …

Extension reading

From *Toro! Toro!* By Michael Morpurgo

This story is set in Andalucia, Spain, in 1936. Antonito lives on his parents' bull farm where he rides his horse, Chica, and looks after a little bull calf called Paco. Life is good until he discovers that Paco is going to be sent to the bullring when he is big enough. Antonito knows well that the end of the fight with a *matador* always ends in the bull's death. Antonito cannot bear to think that his beloved Paco will die that way, and he plans to run away from his parents' farm, and take Paco with him. But in 1936 a civil war was being fought in Spain, and Antonito does not realize the danger he and his family are in.

🔊 Toro! Toro! 🔊

That same night I lay in my bed forcing myself to stay awake. I waited until the house fell silent about me, until I was as sure as I could be that everyone was asleep. The sound of Father's deep snoring was enough to convince me that it was
5   safe to move.

I was already dressed under my blankets. I stole out of the house and across the moonlit yard towards the stable. The dogs whined at me, but I patted them and they did not bark. I led Chica out of her stable, mounting her some way down
10 the farm track, out of sight of the house, and then rode out over the farm towards Paco's corral.

My idea was clumsy but simple. I knew that to separate Paco from the others, to release him on his own would be almost impossible, and that even if I succeeded, sooner or later he
15 would be bound to come running back to the others. He was after all a herd animal. I would have to release them all, all of them together, and drive them as far as I could up into the cork forests where they could lose themselves and never be found. Even if they caught a few of them, Paco might be
20 lucky. At least this way he stood some chance of avoiding the horrors of the *corrida*.

The cattle shifted in the corral as I came closer. They were nervous, unsettled by this straight night-time visitor. I dismounted at the gate and opened it. For some while they
25 stood looking at me, snorting, shaking their horns. I called out quietly into the night. 'Paco! Paco! It's me. It's Antonito!'

I knew he would come, and he did, walking slowly towards me, his ears twitching and listening all the time as I sweetened
30 him closer. Then, as he reached the open gate, the others began to follow. It all happened so fast after that. To begin with, they came at a gentle walk through the gate. Then they were trotting, then jostling, then galloping, charging past me. Paco, I felt sure, was gone with them, swept along in the
35 stampede.

I don't know what it was that knocked me senseless, only that when I woke, I was not alone. Paco was standing over me, looking down at me, and Chica was grazing nearby. Whether Paco had saved me from being trampled to death,
40 I do not know. What I did know was that my plan had worked perfectly, better than I could ever have hoped for.

I got to my feet slowly, amazed that nothing was broken. I was not badly hurt at all, just a little bruised, and my cheek was cut. I could feel the blood sticky under my hand when
45 I touched it. I had no rope, but I knew I would not need one, that Paco would follow along behind Chica and me as if he'd been trained to it.

I had in mind to go as far as I could, as fast as I could, before dawn. Beyond that I had no thought as to where we would
50 go, nor what I would do with him. As we climbed the rutty tracks up into the hills, I felt inside me a sudden surge of elation. Paco was free and now I would keep him free. I had no conscience any more about what I had done, no thought now of what it would mean to Father to lose his precious
55 herd of cattle. Paco would not suffer that terrible death in the ring – that was all that mattered to me. I had done it, and I was ecstatic.

Chica seemed to know the path, and she was as surefooted as a mule. I never once came near to falling off, despite my exhaustion. Behind us, Paco was finding it more difficult, but he was managing.

I felt the damp of the morning mist around us before I ever saw the dawn. We climbed on, higher and higher into the mist, until the last of the night was gone and a hazy white sun rose over the hills.

We came suddenly into a clearing. On the far side was a stone hut, most of it in ruins, and beside it a circular stone corral. I hadn't seen this one before, but I had seen others. There were several like it scattered through the cork forests, built for gathering cattle or sheep or goats. Paco followed us in and I shut the gate behind him. Both Paco and Chica at once began nuzzling the grass. I lay down in the shelter of the wall, and was asleep before I knew it.

The warming sun woke me, that or the cry of the vultures. They were circling above us in the blue. The mist had all gone. Paco lay beside me, chewing the cud and licking his nose. Chica stood, resting her fourth leg, only half awake. I lay there for a while, trying to gather my thoughts.

That was when I heard the sound of distant droning, like a million bees. There were no bees to be seen, and nothing else either. I thought I must be imagining things, but then Paco was on his feet and snorting. The vultures were suddenly gone. The droning was coming closer, ever closer, until it became a throbbing angry roar that filled the air about us. Then I saw them, flying low over the ridge towards us, dozens of them: airplanes with black crosses on their wings. They came right over us, their engines thunderous, throbbing so loudly that it hurt my ears.

In my terror I curled up against the wall and covered my ears. Paco was going wild and Chica, too, was circling the corral, looking for a way out. I waited until the planes were gone, then climbed up on to the wall of the corral. They were diving now, their engines screaming, diving on Sauceda, diving on my home.

95   I saw the smoke of the first bombs before I heard the distant crunch of the explosions. It was as if some vengeful God was pounding the village with his fist, each punch sending up a plume of fire, until the whole village was covered in a pall of smoke.

100   I stood there on the corral walk, trying not to believe what my eyes were telling me. They were telling me that my whole world was being destroyed, that Father and Mother and Maria were down there somewhere in that smoke and fire. I don't think I really believed it until the planes had gone, 105   until I heard the sound of silence again, and then the sound of my own crying.

MICHAEL MORPURGO

Comprehension

1   Why is Antonito running away?

2   What does he plan to do to save Paco?

3   What happens to Antonito's village?

4   What do you think the black crosses stand for?

5   What symbolic role do you think the vultures play?

Talking points

1   Do you think that bullfighting is a cruel sport?

2   Do you think Antonito was justified in his actions?

3   How does the bombing change the focus of the story?

Changing places

8

What happens when you move to another part of the world?

In this unit you will:

Experience
- the Statue of Liberty
- an Afghan refugee camp
- migrating birds
- immigration to the USA, the UK and Australia

Read
- prose fiction
- a poem
- a letter
- an autobiographical essay

Create
- journal entries
- a letter
- a poster

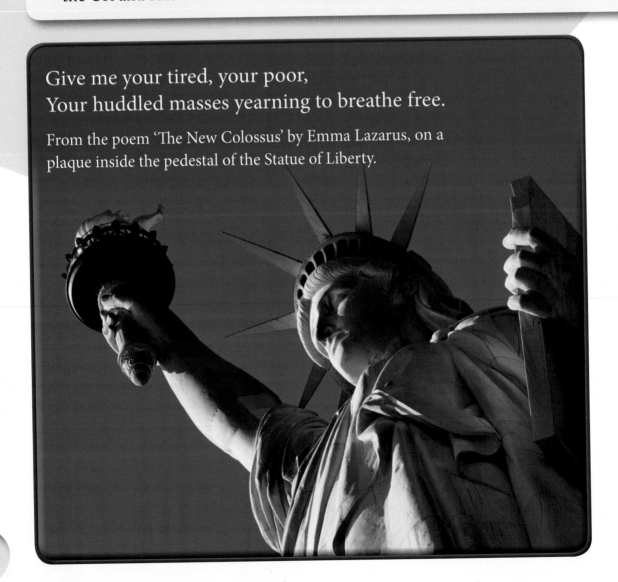

Give me your tired, your poor,
Your huddled masses yearning to breathe free.

From the poem 'The New Colossus' by Emma Lazarus, on a plaque inside the pedestal of the Statue of Liberty.

The Statue of Liberty

The statue of 'Liberty Enlightening The World' was erected on Ellis Island in New York harbour in 1886. It was a gift of friendship from the French people to commemorate the part they played in the American Revolution and the Declaration of Independence. It has stood ever since as a 'universal symbol of freedom and democracy'. It has traditionally been seen as a symbol of hope to all immigrants who came to New York to start a new life in America.

Word origins

The words 'emigration', 'immigration' and 'migration', and the verb 'to migrate', all come from the Latin verb *migrare*, which means 'to move from one place to another'.

Talking points

1 Have you always lived in the country you are in now?

2 Has anyone in your circle of family and friends gone to another country to start a new life?

The Statue of Liberty with New York City in the background.

Journal

Write a journal entry about the day you arrived in your new country. If not based on personal experience, interview a friend or relative, and describe their experience.

Toolkit

You looked at prefixes in Unit 6 (page 102). The prefixes e- and im- in 'emigration' and 'immigration' come from Latin. The prefix ex- or e- means 'out of', and in- means 'into'. When the prefix in- comes before a word beginning with 'm', the in changes to im: 'immigration'.

- Make a list of English words you know that have ex-, e-, in- or im- at the beginning.

- Are any of them words that you can use without the ex-, e-, in- or im- prefix? **W**

A new life in America

All new immigrants to America in the first half of the twentieth century had to go to the Ellis Island immigration station, a short ferry ride from Liberty Island and New York City. From 1892 to 1954, 17 million people passed through Ellis Island.

1907, the year this photo was taken, was the peak year for immigration at Ellis Island with 1,004,756 people processed. Generally, those immigrants who were approved spent from two to five hours on the island. People with obvious health problems were held in the island's hospital facilities for a period of time. They all had to answer 29 questions, including their name, age, occupation (job) and how much money they had on them. Some immigrants were rejected outright and sent back where they came from.

An Italian immigrant family at Ellis Island, New York, waiting to be processed after their long sea voyage.

It has been estimated that nearly half of all Americans today can trace their family history to at least one person who passed through the Port of New York at Ellis Island.

Talking points

1 Discuss with your group what it must feel like to move to another part of the world.

2 Look at the pictures on the next page of people and animals from around the world, and read what the people are saying.

3 Describe the situation in each picture.

Ellis Island, with Liberty Island in the background.

Life in pictures

'I can't earn enough money here to keep my family'.

'We're starting a new life here in America.'

'Look at the Snow Geese in perfect V formation. They have flown a long way to get here from the Arctic.'

'Should we ask Shareen if she wants to join us? It feels a bit awkward.'

Prose fiction

**From *Mud City* by
Deborah Ellis**

People do not always choose to emigrate. Many people are forced to leave their home because of violence or war. The following story is about Shauzia, a 12-year-old girl who left Afghanistan after conflict made her country unsafe. She travelled across the border to a refugee camp in Pakistan, but she hated life in the camp. She dreamed of travelling to France and starting a new life. With her dog Jasper for company, Shauzia left the camp to follow her dream, and reaches the city of Peshawar. Disguised as a boy, she looks for work.

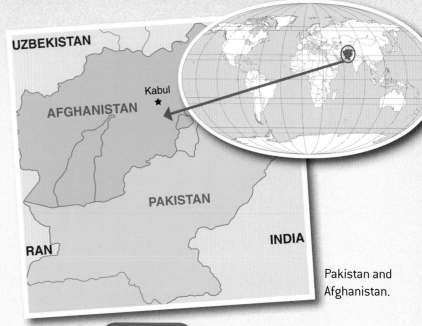

Pakistan and Afghanistan.

❦ Shauzia's Dream ❦

Shauzia tried hard to find a job. She did many different ones, some lasting a few days, some just a few hours. In the cloth market, with rainbows of fabrics hanging over the walkway like a multicoloured forest, she helped unload the heavy bolts
5 of cloth, and put buttons into jars.

She cleaned the butcher's shop, and one day she set up sheep's heads on the table outside. The butcher gave her a good-sized bone for Jasper at the end of that day. He also recommended her to his friend who had a grocer's shop, and she got a day's
10 work there, cleaning the floor.

She got a few days' work delivering cups of tea while the tea shop's regular delivery boy was sick. She delivered trays of tea to merchants who couldn't leave their shops for a break. She was good at it, too, and could hurry through the narrow
15 streets of the market without spilling a drop. Everywhere

Wordpool

Discuss the meaning of the following words taken from the extract.

fabrics (line 3)
narrow (14)
furniture (17)
counter (21)
bundle (26)
Make your own word pool of any other unfamiliar words.

she delivered tea, she asked if there was work for her. She was rewarded with a job sweeping out a furniture warehouse.

One day, instead of looking for work, she went to the train
20 station. 'Do any of these trains go to the sea?' she asked the man behind the ticket counter.

The ticket seller told her the price of a single ticket to the port city of Karachi. It was much, much more than she had saved. She turned away sadly and was almost back on the
25 street when a man gave her a tip of a few rupees to carry his bundle to the train.

After that, on the days when she didn't have other jobs, she went to the train station and carried people's bags for tips. She couldn't go there often because the regular porters who
30 were officially employed chased her away if they saw her.

It was just as well. She found it hard watching other people get on the trains when she longed to do so herself. When would it be her turn?

Each night she added more rupees to the soft purse hung
35 around her neck. Each night she felt she was a little closer to the sea.

DEBORAH ELLIS

Toolkit

Did you notice the words with *apostrophes*? Explain why apostrophes are used in the following words, and why they are placed where they are:

butcher's (line 6)

day's (line 9)

people's (line 28)

couldn't (line 29).

Talking points

1 Which of Shauzia's jobs would you least like to do?

2 Do you think that Shauzia's dream of going to Europe will come true?

3 Have you ever had a dream which did or did not come true?

Comprehension

1 Why does Shauzia hang her purse around her neck?

2 What do you think carrying people's bags 'for tips' means? (line 25)

3 Why do you think Shauzia finds it 'hard' watching other people get on the trains? (line 31)

4 What does this final sentence tell you about how Shauzia felt? (line 35)

5 Why does Shauzia turn away sadly after speaking to the ticket seller?

Life on the wing

It is not just people who move from one country to another. Many birds migrate between continents. Did you know that swallows migrating from Europe to central Africa fly 200 miles a day at a speed of 17–22 miles per hour? Their maximum speed is 35 miles per hour. It is not surprising that migration is a hazardous time for the birds. Many die of starvation and exhaustion, or in storms.

Swallows gathered on telephone lines in the UK, preparing to migrate.

A hobby falcon is a bird of prey and an enemy to migrating swallows.

Prose fiction

from *Dear Olly* by Michael Morpurgo

In this story the swallows return each year to nest in a family's garage in England. Brother and sister Matt and Olly watch them each year as they nest, lay their eggs and raise their young. But this year Olly is alone, because her brother, Matt, is in Africa. When one of the baby swallows is injured by a neighbour's cat, Olly and her mother nurse it back to health. It is then able to join the other swallows on their migration at the end of the summer. Olly calls the swallow Hero, and hopes that it will find her brother in Africa. This part of the story describes the beginning of Hero's long and hazardous journey.

Wordpool

expectancy (line 7)

terror (13)

swifter (16)

to swerve (20)

to swirl (28)

৩ Hero's Journey ৫

Hero joined the others as they flocked to a nearby lake, and for several days he hunted there, skimming over the water after mosquitoes. He was safe here with his family, amongst thousands upon thousands of gathering swallows and martins.

5 All the while, his strength grew within him. At dusk as darkness began to fall, they gathered to roost in the trees around the lake. Every night in the roost the air of expectancy grew. Every night the birds were slower to settle to their sleep.

10 Then one morning early, the hobby falcon came gliding high over the lake. The birds heard his killer kew-kew call and scattered in terror.

Down came
the hobby falcon,
15 swifter than any bird Hero
had ever seen.
Hero felt the wind of
him as he passed by,
and swerved aside only
20 just in time. But the hobby falcon
was not after him, he was
after a young martin, slower
and more stuttering in flight than
Hero – and for the martin there
25 was no escape.

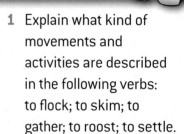

The flock flew that same morning. A whispering cloud of birds swirled out over the lake; the sky darkened as it went. They flew south towards the sea, hoping that they had seen the last of the hobby falcon. But the hobby falcon was not
30 far behind, for he too was bound for Africa. He would fly all the way with them, taking the youngest, the slowest, the weakest, whenever he felt like it. He had done it before.

MICHAEL MORPURGO

Looking closely

1 Explain what kind of movements and activities are described in the following verbs: to flock; to skim; to gather; to roost; to settle.

2 The movements of the hobby falcon are different from those of the swallows. Which words help you to imagine the hobby falcon's movements?

3 Why is the hobby falcon so frightening to the migrating birds? How does the line spacing add to the effect?

4 In the final paragraph there are so many birds that they look like a cloud. Why do you think the author describes the cloud as 'whispering'? What caused the sky to darken?

5 What happens to the birds that don't make it all the way to Africa?

Who is an alien?

The noun 'alien' is a word for a person from a very different family, people, or place. It is also used to mean a creature from outer space! Have you ever felt like an alien? You may be able to identify with some of the feelings in the following poem.

Poetry

The writer uses the idea of an alien from outer space to describe how she felt as a schoolgirl when she emigrated to England.

❧ Alien Abduction ❧

Snatched away on a not quite round silver saucer
To a world unknown, far away and alien
To me.

Abducted from my world.
5   What for?
'For your own good, for education, for ...'
They said.

They called this world England:
Small, contained, powerful
10 And surrounded by sea.

A solitary world inside a world –
Like me.

One of my kind –
Or so I felt.
15 Searching eyes and hostile glances
Scoured me each and every day,
Questioning my right to be here.

I was different:
A black-haired, brown-eyed
20 Blot in a white sea.

It took time for me to understand
That, alien as this country was to me,
An alien is what I was to them.
Would I ever be anything else?

MARIYA AZIZ

Wordpool

saucer   solitary (11)
(line 1)   hostile (15)
to abduct (4)   to scour (16)

Looking closely

1 Why do you think the poet calls the poem 'Alien Abduction'?

2 Who do you think 'they' refers to in line 7?

3 The poet uses the word 'alien' more than once. Why do you think she repeats it?

4 How does 'a world unknown' compare with 'my world'? (lines 2 and 4)

5 What does the writer understand by the last four lines of the poem?

Writing a letter

Here is a letter which a grandmother in Delhi in India wrote to her granddaughter in the UK, after the granddaughter had emigrated there with her family.

> Apt 3, Block A,
> Shanti Bhavan
> Lodhi Road
> Delhi 110003
>
> 15 October
>
> Dear Shenaz,
>
> You have been in England for six months now and I miss you more each day. I hope that you have settled into your new school now and that you are enjoying it. I am sure that you are working hard because you are such a good girl. You must work hard and take advantage of the opportunities in your new country and make your parents proud of you.
>
> Please write and tell me all about your new life. Have you made some new friends? What is the town of Leicester like? The buildings must be very different. I cannot imagine them. I am busy every day, but I am always thinking about my dear family so far away.
>
> Look after your mother and father and little sisters for me. I long to give you a big hug.
>
> With lots of love from
> Ammamamma

Pretend that you are a young person who has emigrated to another country, and you are writing a reply to a letter from your grandmother, or other relative.

A new life in Australia

What do you know about the history of emigration to Australia? The 2001 census in Australia showed that the people came from more than 200 countries

According to the Australian Government, 6.4 million migrants have arrived in the country since 1945. A large proportion of these immigrants arrived in the immediate post-war period. The Second World War (1939–45) had left many Europeans displaced and homeless.

Many people also left Europe voluntarily to start a new life. Between 1945 and 1972, Australia ran the Assisted Passage Scheme to encourage people from the United Kingdom to emigrate. British people paid only £10 pounds for their fare, but had to stay for at least two years. Most travelled by boat, but some paid the difference to travel by air rather than sea. The photograph below is of families waving goodbye at London Airport in 1948.

Analysing the impact of a poster

The picture below is a poster designed in 1948 to encourage people in Britain to emigrate to Australia. What do you think people looking at the poster would imagine Australia was like?

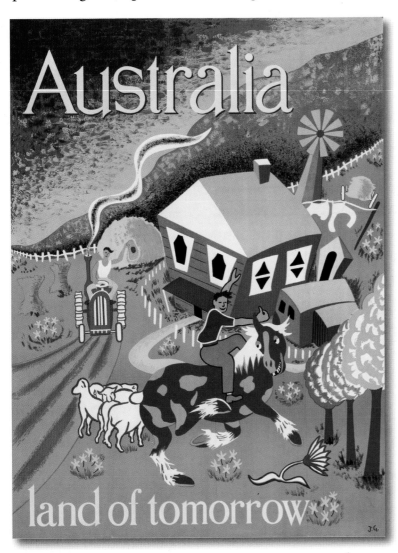

Designing a poster

Keep in mind the things you noticed about the Australian poster shown above. Use the ideas from your discussion to help you create a successful design for a poster of your own.

- Make a poster to encourage new emigrants to come to a country.
- It may be the country where you were born, the country you are now living in, or any other country.
- Think of a slogan (a vivid phrase or sentence that promotes a message, as in 'land of tomorrow') for your poster.

Talking points

1 Describe the life being advertised in this poster. What is going on? What is the mood of the scene?

2 What do you think 'land of tomorrow' means?

3 How successful do you think this poster is? Is it a convincing image of Australia?

Autobiographical essay

**From *The Relative Advantages of Learning My Language*
by Amy Choi**

In the following extract, Amy Choi remembers her grandfather. Amy emigrated with her family, including her grandfather, from China to Australia as a child.

❧ Grandfather's Language ❧

I was never particularly kind to my grandfather. He was my mother's father, and he lived with us when I was a teenager. I remember him coming into the sitting room one night, and when he went to sit down, I said to my brother, 'I hope he
5 doesn't sit down.' I didn't think my grandfather understood much English, but he understood enough, and as I watched, he straightened up again, and without a word, returned to his room. I was twelve years old.

My grandfather wrote poetry on great rolls of thin white
10 paper with a paintbrush. He offered to read and explain his poems to me several times over the years, but I only let him do it once. I'd let my Chinese go by then, which made listening to him too much of an effort. Though I was raised speaking Chinese, it wasn't long before I lost my language skills. I
15 spoke English all day at school, listened to English all night on TV. I didn't see the point of speaking Chinese. We lived in Australia.

From Monday to Friday, Grandad went to the city, dressed in a suit with a waistcoat, a hat, and carrying his walking
20 stick. He would take the bus to the station, the train to the city, then the tram to Little Bourke Street. On Mondays, he'd be sitting at a large round table at Dragon Boat Restaurant with other old Chinese men. Tuesdays to Fridays, he was at a small square table by himself with a pot of tea and the
25 Chinese newspaper. I watched him leave in the morning and come back in the afternoon, as punctual and as purposeful as any school child or office worker, for years.

GLOSSARY

The author uses some expressions commonly used in speech, but not in formal written English:

I'd let my Chinese go means 'I had allowed myself to forget most of my Chinese'.

Could barely string a sentence together means 'had great difficulty speaking even a sentence'.

Whenever I am stuck for a word means 'whenever I cannot think of a word'.

Throw into a conversation means 'use in a conversation'.

Wordpool

waistcoat (line 19)

funeral (28)

to compliment (32)

to master (46)

to ensure (49)

When Amy was sixteen, her grandfather died.

At the funeral, my sadness was overshadowed by a sense of regret. I'd denied my grandfather the commonest of kindnesses.
30 I was sixteen years old. I am now twenty-six. A few weeks ago, during a family dinner at a Chinese restaurant, the waiter complimented my mother on the fact that I was speaking to her in Chinese. The waiter told Mum with a sigh that his own children could barely string a sentence together in
35 Chinese. Mum told the waiter I had stopped speaking Chinese a few years into primary school, but that I had suddenly started up again in my late teens.

I have often wondered how aware my mum is of the connection between Grandad's death and my improving Chinese. Whenever
40 I am stuck for a word, I ask her. Whenever I am with her, or relatives, or a waiter at a Chinese restaurant, or a sales assistant at a Chinese department store, I practise. I am constantly adding new words to my Chinese vocabulary, and memorising phrases I can throw into a conversation. It is my
45 way of re-learning a language. Textbooks and teachers are not necessary, since I am only interested in mastering the spoken word. I am not trying to 'discover my roots'. I am simply trying to ensure that the next time an elderly relative wants me to listen, I am not only willing, I am able.

AMY CHOI

Talking points

1 In what ways did Amy and her grandfather adapt differently to living in another country?

2 Why do you think Amy's views about her language changed?

3 Do you know people who have adapted to a new life in different ways? What were their experiences?

4 What do you think of Amy's ways of re-learning her language?

Journal

Write a journal entry on the different languages you know and what impact they have on your daily life.

Comprehension

1 Describe Amy's act of unkindness when she was 12.

2 Why didn't Amy want to listen to her grandfather talking about his poems?

3 Explain the ways in which Amy's grandfather remained Chinese while he was living in Australia.

4 How did Amy feel at her grandfather's funeral?

5 How did her grandfather's death affect Amy's attitude to learning the Chinese language?

9 Identity

How do we see others and ourselves?

In this unit you will:

Experience
- Native Americans: Quechan and Navaho people
- The Middle East
- Papua New Guinea

Read
- fables
- prose fiction
- autobiography
- poetry
- an editorial

Create
- a journal entry
- a fable
- a composition
- a prose poem
- a class recital
- a debate

I note the obvious differences
between each sort and type,
but we are more alike, my friends,
than we are unalike.

From 'Human Family'
by Maya Angelou

Talking points

1 Who are you? What makes you different from or similar to others?

2 Maya Angelou's poem says there are different 'sorts' and 'types' of people. What 'sorts' and 'types' do you know?

3 Think of all the people around the world. Think of your family and friends. What is similar or different about them?

4 How would you identify yourself in a crowd, or in your class or family?

In this quoted extract from a poem, the American writer Maya Angelou points out that there are many similarities and differences between people. This is often the cause of conflict. But, by drawing attention to the fact that we are 'more alike' than 'unalike', she supports the idea that we should live together in harmony.

What do fables tell us about identity?

A fable is a simple story which can be understood on a metaphorical level. It is a story with a moral. This means that it has a message in it that will teach you something about human behaviour. Many stories in fables are about animals, but the moral is about human behaviour. Fables often include ideas about people's identity, as individuals and as communities. In this chapter there are three examples.

Talking points

1 What kind of messages do these fables have for us?

2 Can you think of good titles for each of them?

3 Discuss the morals in these fables. An example of a moral is: 'If you are cruel, you will never be happy'.

The Bremen Town Musicians, from Grimm's Fairytales.

Toolkit

Focus on vocabulary

alike / like / unalike (adj) We are more *alike*, my friends, than we are *unalike*

similar (adj) *similarity* (noun) *similarly* (adv)

different (adj) *difference* (noun)

comparison/contrast (noun); *to compare, to contrast* (verb) W

Journal

Describe yourself. How are you different, and how are you similar to other people that you know?

Fable 1
Retold from *The Obvious Elephant* **by Bruce Robinson**

❧ The Obvious Elephant ❧

One day long ago, the people of a village woke to find a huge, grey animal in the middle of their field. No one knew what it was or how it had got there. The children ran round it excitedly, and prodded it with sticks. One of them poked
5   it in the eye. The grown-ups laughed as they, too, prodded the poor animal. Some villagers were afraid of the strange monster and went back indoors. Someone threw a stone. At that moment, the Professor came along.

'Stop all this immediately!' he ordered. 'I will find out what
10   this animal is.'

The Professor went to his library and found out.

'It's an ELEPHANT!' he told the villagers.

'Oh! That's what it is! It's an ELEPHANT!' cried the villagers.

15   And when they knew what he was, they made him welcome. They made him a necklace of flowers for his huge neck and gave him a name. From then on the villagers looked after the elephant and they lived together happily ever after.

BRUCE ROBINSON

Wordpool

Discuss the meaning of the following words taken from the extract.

obvious (title)

to prod (line 5)

Make your own wordpool of any other unfamiliar words you come across.

Obviously, it's an elephant!

Fable 2

This is a traditional story told by the Quechan people, who are Native Americans from the lower Colorado River in Arizona, USA.

ಶಿ A Quechan fable ಣಾ

They say dogs used to talk just like people. Dogs lived with their Indian masters, spoke the Indian language and talked all the time. The only trouble was that the dogs talked too much. They never stopped. Whenever anything happened

5 – they told it. Whatever they heard, they told it. Whatever they saw, they told it. The dogs told everything. No one could keep a secret; no one could hide anything.

So the Indians got together and spoke to the Great Spirit, 'Great Spirit, hear our prayer. Do something about these

10 dogs of ours. We cannot keep secrets any more.'

But the dogs went on telling what they saw and heard. Each night the people went to bed worrying about what secrets the dogs would be telling when they woke up.

Then, one morning an old man stood up and shoved his dog.

15 'Well, dog,' he said. 'Go and tell everybody I shoved you!'

The dog just looked at him for a minute but said nothing. The old man was surprised. He tried something else. He whispered a secret. Then he said, 'Well, dog, go ahead and tell everybody my secret.'

20 Again the dog just looked at him but he didn't say a word. He didn't tell the secret. Instead he BARKED. He just barked. What a relief! The Indian people knew that the Great Spirit had found a way to answer their prayers.

Now dogs bark a lot. Whenever they see a person coming

25 into an Indian village they bark. When they hear a sound at night they bark. They always bark, but they don't tell secrets any more.

So you'd better be careful what you say. You might end up having to bark.

Wordpool

to shove (line 14)
relief (22)

Fable 3

෨ A fable by Aesop ๖

There was once a man and a lion who were travelling together on a long journey. As they walked along, they talked about many things. The lion boasted that he was stronger and braver than a man, and the man boasted that he was stronger
5   and braver than a lion.

'Of course, a man is stronger than a lion,' boasted the man. 'Think of all the battles they have won!'

'Of course, a lion is stronger than a man,' boasted the lion, 'Think how much bigger the lion is!'

10   As they continued to argue, they came to a crossroads where there was a statue of a man strangling a lion.

'There you are!' cried the man. 'Is that not proof that a man is stronger than a lion?'

'Wait a moment, wait a moment,' said the lion. 'That is just
15   your view. If we lions could make statues, I am sure we would see the lion winning the fight!'

Wordpool

to boast [line 3]

crossroads [10]

to strangle [11]

statue [15]

Writing a fable

Now it is your turn to write a fable. Your discussion should have given you some ideas for a message or moral for a fable.

- What kind of moral would you like to illustrate?
- Think of an appropriate setting. Keep your story simple.
- Decide on your characters. You might want to include animals, or people from different backgrounds.

Talking points

1 What does fable 1 tell you about how human beings behave when they meet something unfamiliar?

2 What does each of the fables tell you about identity?

3 What happens when we know more about other living beings?

What is the identity of a community?

For many people, their identity is strongly bound up with their country or where they live. This means that feeling a part of their country or community is very important to them.

Prose fiction

From *Sing Down the Moon* by Scott O'Dell

The following text is set in the early 1860s, in the United States. In this extract, the young Navaho girl Bright Morning has been captured by Spanish slavers, who are negotiating her price with a white landowner. At the time in which the story is set, the Navaho people were being driven from their lands, and their communities broken up.

Navaho Indians crossing the Canyon de Chelly in the early twentieth century.

ᔑ Captured ᔐ

She walked around me, gently running her hand across my back. Then she asked me to smile and when I refused she reached out and pushed my lips back with her fingers. On one side I have a broken tooth, which happened when I was
5   very young and fell against a stone.

The woman made a sound with her tongue, but said nothing. Then she walked around me once more and left the room with the Spaniard.

The girl, who had opened the gate for us and who was stirring
10   the beans, said, 'My name is Rosita. I am twelve years old and I come from the White Mesa, in the Navajo country. What is your name? Where do you come from? How old are you?'

I told her one of my names, but not my real one. 'I am fifteen
15   and I come from the Canyon de Chelly.'

'I have never heard of that place,' Rosita said.

This surprised me, for I thought everyone had heard of the Canyon de Chelly. 'It is the most beautiful place in the world,' I said. 'It has the most sheep and the finest wool. It has a
20   river and tall cliffs that catch the sun and make the melons grow bigger than pumpkins. There the cornstalks grow taller than you are.'

I wanted to tell her more about the Canyon de Chelly, but my throat filled up with sadness.

25   Rosita put a bowl of beans and chili on the table beside me, where I could reach it.

'You will be happy here,' she said. 'The lady is kind and her husband also. He is a soldier and does not come here often, mostly on feast days. There is good food to eat and the work
30   is not hard. It will be nicer when you are in the house. The other girl I do not like. She is a Zuni.'

Wordpool

to refuse (2)

cliffs (20)

throat (24)

to haggle (34)

to weave (46)

GLOSSARY

A **mesa** is a Spanish word for a high, flat plateau (a flat-topped hill).

Adobe is a Spanish name for bricks dried in the sun.

Anglos, short for 'Anglo-Saxons', means English people.

A **hogan** is a traditional Navajo house.

A **canyon** is a valley enclosed by steep natural rock walls.

From the next room I heard the sound of the woman and the Spaniard talking. They talked like the Anglos who come to our canyon and haggle over the price of wool. Rosita
35 listened to them for a moment. 'The Senora paid little for me,' she said. 'But for you she will pay more. You are pretty and tall. I wish you were my sister.'

After a long time the Spaniard left. He was carrying a leather pouch. It was filled with coins that jingled.

40 'I told you,' Rosita said. 'The pouch is twice as full as it was for me.'

The woman came and led me out of the kitchen. My black dog was waiting for me. We went along a path to a smaller house far in the back. It had a wide, blue door and inside
45 was a room bigger than our hogan and home, where all my family lived, cooking and weaving rugs and sleeping. The floor was not made of common earth like ours, but of adobe mixed with blood. It was smooth and dark and and on it were two Navajo blankets.

50 'You sleep there,' the woman told me, pointing to a big bed. She spoke to me in Navajo. Her words had a strange sound but I understood them. She opened the doors of an empty cupboard. 'For clothes,' she said. 'Tomorrow I buy you shoes, dresses, and some ribbons for your hair.'

SCOTT O'DELL

Talking points

1 What do you think of the Navajo Indian names, like Bright Morning?

2 What names would you give yourself and other people you know?

3 Do names in your family mean something in your language?

4 What do you know about the Navajo people?

Comprehension

1 What happens to Bright Morning in the opening of the extract?

2 Why is Bright Morning surprised that Rosita has not heard of the Canyon de Chelly?

3 Why do you think Bright Morning does not tell Rosita her real name?

4 Why does Rosita wish she was her sister?

5 What kind of work will Bright Morning be required to do?

Looking closely

1 What is the meaning of the word 'haggle'? [line 34]

2 What colour would adobe bricks mixed with blood be? [line 47]

3 Why does the woman's Navajo sound strange? [line 51]

What does it mean to have more than one identity?

As you saw in unit 8, people's sense of their own identity can be complicated if they or their families have moved to different countries. It can be difficult living in a country with different traditions to the ones you have grown up with.

Autobiography

From *Introduction to 19 Varieties of Gazelle: Poems of the Middle East* by Naomi Shihab Nye

Naomi Shihab Nye is an Arab-American poet. She was born in America, but you can see from what she writes about herself that her family still identifies closely with the Middle East.

ᔥ A Flavour of the Middle East ᔦ

All my life I thought about the Middle East, wrote about it, wondered about it, lived in it, visited it, worried about it, loved it. We are blessed and doomed at the same time.

5 I was born in the United States, but my father stared back toward the Middle East whenever he stood outside. Our kitchen smelled like the Middle East – garlic and pine nuts sizzled in olive oil, fried eggplant, hot pita bread. My father dropped sprigs of mint into our pots of hot tea. He had been happy as a boy in the Old City of Jerusalem with his Palestinian
10 and Greek and Jewish and Armenian neighbors. But after the sad days of 1948, when his family lost their home and everything they owned, he wanted to go away. He was one of the few foreign university students in Kansas in the 1950s, and was a regular customer at the local drugstore soda
15 fountain in his new little town.

'He always looked dreamy, preoccupied, like he could see things other people couldn't see,' the druggist told me twenty-five years later. Well yes, I thought. That's what immigrants look like. They always have other worlds in their minds.

20 My father and my American mother invented new dishes using Middle Eastern ingredients. We were proud without

GLOSSARY

Eggplant is another name for the vegetable also known as aubergine or brinjal.

Pita bread, also spelled 'pitta', is a flat bread traditional in Middle Eastern and Mediterranean cuisine.

Wordpool

doomed (line 3)
to sizzle (7)
sprigs (8)
preoccupied (16)
to camp out (27)

144

knowing it. Travelers from the Middle East often sat in circles in our backyard sharing figs and peaches and speaking in Arabic. Arabic music played in our house. Our father told
25 better folk stories than anyone else's father – he had a gentle wit and almost never got mad. So kids from the neighborhood would camp out on our screened-in back porch, and we would all beg my father to tell more funny stories. It was a rich world to be in.

Naomi Shihab Nye

Looking closely

With a partner, read through the text again and discuss the ways in which the writer and her family keep the Middle East in their lives even though they are living in America.

Toolkit

Because the writer has been brought up in America, she uses American spelling and expressions. In British English, 'neighbour' has a 'u'.

- Can you find any other American spellings in the text?

- The writer mentions the 'drugstore' and the 'soda fountain'. Which words would British English use for these American English words?

- Can you find any more examples of American English vocabulary? **W**

Writing memories

Now try writing about your own memories of moving from one place to another. Write about places that at first seem quite strange and that have since become familiar to you.

- Is there somewhere that you would like to go back to?
- The first person 'I' may be you, a member of your family or a character you have made up. The memories may be real or imagined.
- Use the past tense. Plan what to put in each of your paragraphs and think of an interesting way to conclude your composition.

Our parents told us that we would be going to live in the United Kingdom. We felt a bit scared but also excited at the idea.

Poetry

Some people identify strongly with their country or community. What happens if you feel that you do not belong to any country? That is what the following poem is about.

❧ Citizen of the World ❧

When you are very small
maybe not quite born
your parents move
for some reason you may never
5 understand they move
from their own town
from their own land
and you grow up in a place
that is never quite your home

10 and all your childhood people
with a smile or a fist say
you're not from here are you
and part of you says fiercely yes I am
and part of you feels no I'm not
15 I belong to where my parents belonged

but when you go to their town, their country
people there also say
you're not from here are you
and part of you says no I'm not
20 and part of you says fiercely yes I am
and so you grow up both and neither
and belong everywhere and nowhere much the same
both stronger and weaker for the lack of ground
able to fly but not to rest

25 and all over the world, though you feel alone
are millions like you, like a great flock of swallows
soaring or falling exhausted, wings beating the rhythm
of the wind that laughs at fences or frontiers,
whose home is itself, and the whole world it moves over.

DAVE CALDER

1 Why did the author's parents move? Give some possible reasons why they left their home and their country to make a new life elsewhere.

2 What does 'with a smile or a fist' mean? (line 11)

3 Who is the subject of the poem? (What personal pronoun does the author use?) Does this make the person sound confused about his or her identity?

4 Explain the comparison the author makes between people and 'a great flock of swallows'. (lines 26–9)

Talking points

1 Have you ever felt like the person in the poem?

2 How do the person's feelings change in the last stanza?

3 Do you think that the person will get over the problems that he/she faced early on?

4 What do you think the title of the poem means?

Toolkit

Poets are free to write without punctuation if they wish, just as Dave Calder does in this poem.

Use the poem to practise your use of sentence boundaries, by writing out the poem in continuous prose and adding capital letters and full stops.

Add any other punctuation marks you think are necessary.

Class performance of a poem

This poem expresses strong feelings. You are going to prepare to perform the poem by colour coding the different voices in it.

- On a copy of the poem, use three different colours to identify the different voices in it: the narrator, the other people, the young person.
- Choose how these different voices should be read out aloud in your class or group.
- Practise and then perform the poem. Think about how you can use your voices to enhance the reading.

Why is language so important?

In Unit 8 you read about Amy Choi losing and then regaining the ability to speak Chinese. One of the important things which identifies you is the language you speak. Ralph Waldo Emerson (1803–82) was an American philosopher. He said: 'Language is a city. Every human being brought a stone to the building of it.' What do you think he meant by this?

Editorial

Do you know where each of the following four languages is spoken?

* Trumai
* Catawba
* Usku
* Bidyara.

They are just four of the world's 6,500 languages. These four languages are 'minority languages', which means that they are spoken by small numbers of people. Some minority languages have fewer than ten speakers left.

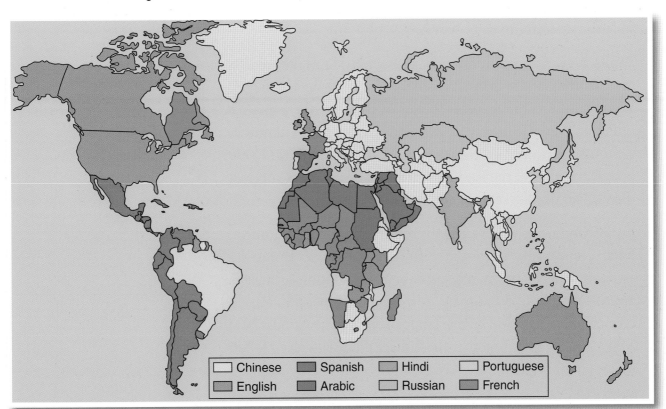

| Chinese | Spanish | Hindi | Portuguese |
| English | Arabic | Russian | French |

Prose non-fiction

From *Vanishing Languages* by David Crystal

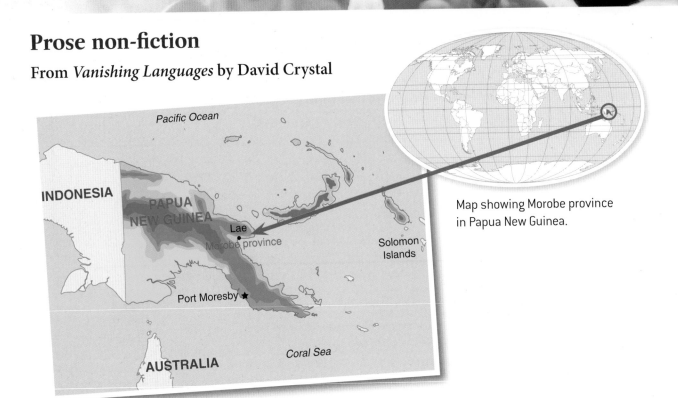

Map showing Morobe province in Papua New Guinea.

১ Vanishing languages ৎ

The deaths of languages are more noticeable in some parts of the world than in others. Where large numbers of languages are concentrated in small geographical regions, the deaths of languages are more obvious.

5 Papua New Guinea, Indonesia and Malaysia make up 2% of the Earth's land area but 25% of the world's living languages! If you travel to the tropical forests of the Morobe province in Papua New Guinea, you will find five isolated villages in a mountain valley. In these villages are fewer than 1,000
10 people who speak the Kapin language. The villagers support themselves and have little contact with outsiders.

In neighbouring valleys there are other tiny communities. Each community speaks a different language. Linguists estimate that in the whole of Papua New Guinea there is
15 approximately one language for every 200 people. Papua New Guinea has 862 living languages; Indonesia has 701; Malaysia has 140. Together these three countries have 1,700 living languages!

The countries' isolation and mountain valleys are two reasons
20 for the existence of so many languages. It is not surprising

Wordpool

noticeable (line 1)
isolated (8)
outsiders (11)
valuable (24)
reserves (24)
consequently (27)

that as remote areas of the world have opened up for trade and tourism, more languages have died. Papua New Guinea has gold, silver and timber. These are valuable reserves, and people
25 come to the islands to make money from them. With them come their own languages, and consequently more Papua New Guinea languages will die and become extinct.

DAVID CRYSTAL

Tari mountain children in Papua New Guinea.

Talking points

1   How many languages are spoken in your class?

2   Do all the languages use an alphabet like the one used in this book?

3   Are they all written from left to right across a page?

4   What makes each of them unique?

Conducting a debate

Linguists believe that in one hundred years' time, half of the world's 6,500 living languages may be extinct. You may think it would be better if one language, a 'global language', was spoken by everyone all over the world. Or you may think that language is an important part of identity and all languages should be kept alive. Have a debate about these issues. The topic, or motion, is: 'We should have one global language'.

- Come up with arguments for and against the statement you are debating.
- Discuss the issues as a class. Remember to listen carefully to others' opinions and add to your own list of arguments.
- Consider all arguments and explain your opinion.
- When you have finished your discussion, vote on the issue. Count how many of you are in favour of one global language, and how many think we should not have one, but many, languages. What have you learned from the debate?

10 Community

How can we make a difference in our communities?

In this unit you will:

Experience
- Thailand
- Mexico
- Staten Island, New York

Read
- poetry
- proverbs
- an interview
- prose fiction

Create
- an essay
- a recipe
- a letter

It was not death or destruction that won that day,
But the human courage
Which shone more golden than the golden sun,
And the human heart
Far deeper than all the waters of the world.

Khunying Chumnongsri Rutnin

The words above are from a poem by the Thai poet Khunying Chumnongsri Rutnin. The poem was read aloud at a memorial service held on 26 December 2005 to remember the 230,000 people who died in the Indian Ocean tsunami one year before. (You read about this tsunami in Unit 4.)

Memorial services were held in all the countries affected by the tsunami. This one was held on Khao Lak beach in Thailand, and the poet's words were spoken by two schoolchildren: one English and one Thai. The English schoolgirl, Tilly Smith, was on the beach on the day of the tsunami. She knew that when the water suddenly disappeared, a great wave would follow, because she had learned about tsunamis at school. Her warnings saved the lives of her family, and about a hundred other people.

Tilly Smith reading the poem.

The power of words

It is difficult to imagine the devastating effects of such a tragedy on the many communities affected by the 2004 tsunami. What do you think the poet's words tell us about the enduring strength of people who are drawn together to help each other out in a crisis?

How can we make a difference in our communities? Sometimes it is through the power of words. Think about this proverb from Madagascar (you looked at a proverb in Unit 5, page 72):

"Words are like eggs: when they hatch they have wings."

When baby birds break out of their eggs, they hatch. This proverb suggests that when words are spoken, they can take on a life of their own. Here is another proverb, from Turkey:

"Kind words unlock an iron door."

Talking points

1 How do you think these proverbs link to the idea of a community?
2 What do you think each tells you about the power of words?
3 How can words be used for good and bad purposes?
4 Is there a proverb you know that you can recite and explain?

Writing an essay

Write an essay about what community means to you. Think about the way communities are defined – sometimes by the street or the suburb in which you live, and other times by nationality or ethnic group, or shared interests. A community can be local or global. Use the following words to help you:

neighbourhood   membership   citizen

kinship   co-operation   society

group   shared interests   identity

Why is friendship important?

Sometimes finding a friend can make all the difference to an individual person. On a larger scale, friendly communities are much better places to live in. The following poem is about the importance of friendship.

✆ Finding a Friend ✆

I could not speak your language
I did not know your rules.
Everything felt foreign
to an alien at school.

5   Those days are long gone now,
though I thought they'd never end.
Now I have no problems
speaking English, making friends.

Dark and haunting memories
10   of loneliness and fear,
frustration and confusion
have begun to disappear.

But one thing I'll remember,
one thing will stay the same.
15   The moment that you smiled at me
and called me by my name.

JANE CLARKE

Wordpool

Discuss the meaning of the following words taken from the poem.

foreign (line 3)

haunting (9)

loneliness (10)

frustration (11)

confusion (11)

Make your own wordpool of any other unfamiliar words you come across.

Toolkit

Rhymes are created by making the last part or parts of a line sound the same. For example, 'thing' and 'bring' rhyme, and 'singing' and 'bringing' also rhyme. In this poem, alternate lines rhyme.

Talking points

1 What difficulties are experienced by the child in the poem?

2 What does the child feel at first?

3 What makes a difference to the child's life?

4 Which line in the poem do you like best?

5 What difference do you think finding a friend makes to someone who is new to the community?

Looking closely

1 How do you think the child feels not being able speak the language or understand the rules of the new country?

2 Write down a word from the poem which means 'stranger'.

3 Why are the child's memories 'Dark and haunting'?

4 Why do you think the child will remember 'The moment that you smiled at me'?

What are community projects?

Sometimes people come together in an organized way to improve things in their communities and make sure that useful work gets done. Below, you will read about one such project in Staten Island, New York.

An interview with Señor Juarez

The interview on the following pages is between a local newspaper reporter and Augustin Juarez, a Mexican immigrant who farms a plot of land on Staten Island. You can see the location of Zapotitlán Lagunas, where Señor Juarez comes from in Mexico, and Staten Island, New York, on the maps below.

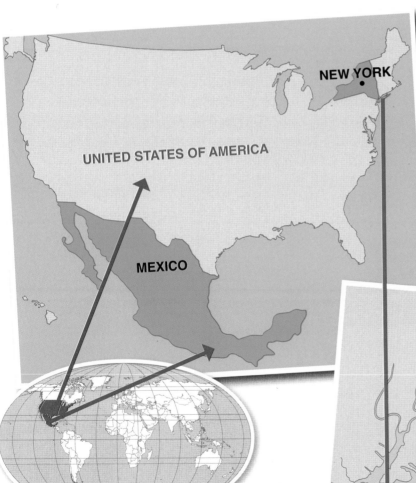

Map showing location of Staten Island, New York and Mexico.

Toolkit

Below are some ways of saying hello in different languages.

Ahlan!	Hallo!
Namaste!	Kalimera!
Hei!	Salud!
Konnichiwa!	Kia ora!
Hola!	Czesc!
Jambo!	Shalom!
Merhaba!	Привет!

Can you identify the languages?

Can you identify the common greeting below?

السلام عليكم

Do you know which language this is?

こんにちは

NEW YORK CITY BOROUGHS

Putting questions and answers into the correct order

The interview has been presented in a jumbled-up way. The newspaper reporter's ten questions are listed under the letters a—j below in the correct order. But Señor Juarez's replies are not. Can you arrange the answers, listed 1—10 on page 157, in the correct order?

Señor Juarez's first language is Spanish. The words he speaks in Spanish are in italics. Can you pronounce his name? Can you translate his words into your own language?

Here are the newspaper reporter's questions (in the correct order):

a Good morning, Mr Juarez. Thank you for letting me write about your experiences as a Mexican immigrant in our local newspaper.

b How long have you been in New York now?

c So you decided to emigrate?

d What was life like for you when you first arrived?

e A life-belt? A very vivid description! What exactly did the Development Project do for you?

f Was it very hard work for you?

g It's certainly an amazing market here with its 600 varieties of produce. What do you sell?

h Who buys your produce?

i So it's genuine Mexican produce. What a great story of determination, hard work and success! New immigrants will be encouraged by your story. Have you any hopes for the future?

j Well, I feel sure that those ambitions will soon be fulfilled. Thank you very much for talking to me, Mr Juarez.

GLOSSARY

Señor is the Spanish term for addressing a man, similar to 'Mr' or 'Sir'.

The noun **produce** means fruits and vegetables grown to eat, for example in gardens or fields.

Buenos días is a Spanish greeting, which translates as 'good day'.

Encantado is a polite way to greet a stranger in Spanish. It is like the English phrase 'Pleased to meet you'.

Adiós is a Spanish word for 'goodbye'.

Si is the Spanish for 'yes'.

Wordpool

vivid (question e)
varieties (g)
determination (i)
ambitions (j)
rubber (answer 4)
ferry (9) **WB**
remedies (10)

1 I came here seven years ago from Mexico. I grew up in a place in southern Mexico called Zapotitlán Lagunas. Ah, those were happy times in my native country, but hard times, too. I left school to help my father and my brothers on our farm, but however hard we worked, we never had enough money.

2 *Buenos días, señor. Encantado.* If your article gives hope to immigrants like me, I am happy to talk to you.

3 You're welcome, *señor. Adiós.*

4 It was hard for me. My English was not good. I wasn't used to a big city and I missed my family. I was lonely. But I was lucky. Very lucky. I was told about a community project in New York which helped immigrant farmers like me. It was called the New Farmer Development Project and to me it was as though I was drowning and someone threw me … what do they call those rubber rings to save a drowning man?

5 It was a difficult decision. But yes, our family decided that because I was the eldest son, I should emigrate to New York. The plan was that I would work hard and then the family would come and join me later.

6 *Si, si.* Oh yes, it was hard work. It's still hard work, but now I have some of my family to help me. I work 60 hours a week in the kitchens of 'Antonio'. It's an Italian restaurant on Staten Island. But my heart isn't in the kitchens! My heart is on my farm with my plants. Every hour God gives me I am digging, planting, watering, weeding, sowing, harvesting … Each week we come here to St George Greenmarket to sell our produce.

7 Indeed yes! Just this. A piece of land of my own. And a tractor!

8 The people there gave me the gift of a new life. The project owns Decker Farm on Staten Island and they gave me a plot of land there, 5,000 square metres. I was back where I love to be – with my hands in God's earth.

9 After two years on Staten Island, I bought an old van and each week we load it up with alache, epazote, pipicha, tomatillos, lettuce, beans and much more, and come over on the ferry to New York City to the market here.

10 Mexicans! Mexicans love their traditional dishes and remedies. I come here and in an hour all my produce has gone! They all know me now and my chillies are the hottest in the market. I joke and say, 'Taste one! If it's not hot enough for you, don't buy!' They always buy! That's because my seeds are the real thing – they come from Mexico.

Mexican vegetables and herbs

- *Alache* is a green-leaf plant essential for Mexican vegetable soup.
- *Epazote* is a herb used for stomach pains.
- *Pipicha* is a spicy herb used in tacos.
- *Tomatillos* are used for salsa verde.

Salsa verde with tortilla crisps.

Tomatillos: Mexican green tomatoes.

Mexican tacos, made using tortilla flatbreads.

Comprehension

1 Describe the help which the New Farmer Development Project gives to Augustín Juarez, and to people like him.

2 Why did Señor Juarez emigrate from Mexico?

3 Why do Señor Juarez's customers like his produce?

4 What sort of man do you think Señor Juarez is? Quote some phrases from the interview which support your opinions.

5 Which adjective does the reporter use which means the same as 'real' or 'authentic'?

Talking points

1 Do you know of a community project set up to help others? You may have read about one, or know of one in your own community.

2 How successful do you think the community project that helped Señor Juarez is?

Writing a recipe

In the previous text, the Mexican immigrants in New York want to buy Señor Juarez's produce to make their favourite Mexican dishes. Countries all over the world have their own traditional dishes. What is your favourite recipe?

- Research your favourite dish and write a recipe – a guide for how to make it and serve it.
- Include a list of ingredients, and describe the way the recipe should be put together. Is there a special sauce? A special mixture of herbs? A special way of cooking?
- Add an element of commentary throughout your recipe, giving tips and suggesting how the dish can best be enjoyed.
- Add a photograph of the dish if you can. You could make copies and share the different recipes in your class.

Chocolate Cake

INGREDIENTS

200g good quality dark chocolate	85g p
About 60% cocoa solids	1/4 ts
200g butter, cut in pieces	200g
1 tbsp instant coffee granules	200g
85g self-raising flour	25g cc

EQUIPMENT

METHOD

1 Butter a 20cm round cake tin (7.5cm d 140C/conventional 160C/ gas 3. Break based pan. Tip in the butter, then mix th and pour into the pan. Warm through o – don't overheat. Or melt in the microw half way through.

2 While the chocolate is melting, mix the cocoa in a big bowl, mixing with your h bowl and stir in the buttermilk.

3 Now pour the melted chocolate mixtur stirring just until everything is well blen sistency. Pour this into the tin and bake a skewer in the centre it should worry if it cracks a bit). Le turn out onto a wire rack

4 When the cake is cold, cu chocolate into small pieces and sugar, and heat until it is about to boil. late. Stir until the chocolate has melte

Notes

Cuts into 14 slices

Preparation and cooking times:
Prep: 30/40 mins
Cook: 1 hr, plus baking and cooling time

Nutrition per serving:

159

The family as community

From *Red Sky in the Morning* by Elizabeth Laird

Can a family be a community? In the following story, Anna sees Ben, her baby brother, for the first time. Ben has been in hospital since his birth and Anna has not yet been able to see him. She and her family know that baby Ben is disabled and will never develop like other children. Anna has been longing to see him.

The arrival of a new baby in a family is a wonderful and challenging time.

❧ Ben comes home ❧

Mum was just settling him down to sleep. She looked much happier than she had for the last few days. She'd been so miserable and bad-tempered and had cried a lot. I'd had a horrible feeling that she might just leave Ben at the hospital
5 and never bring him home. I felt very afraid that she wouldn't love him. And if she didn't love Ben, perhaps she would stop loving me, too.

But when I saw the tenderness on her face, I felt such relief that I could have danced all round the room. I felt as if she'd
10 been a long, long way away, and had come home again.

'Come and see him, Annie,' she said.

I sometimes wonder if I would have loved Ben quite so much if Mum hadn't shown me his feet first. She lifted up the edge of the blanket, and I saw tiny, perfect miniature toes, pink
15 as shells, soft as petals. He must have felt the blanket move, because he stretched them out and curled them up again. I hadn't seen anything so beautiful in my whole life.

Then Mum put the blanket back over his feet, and uncovered his face. I saw him, my little darling brother, for the first time.
20 His eyes were shut, but his mouth was making a sucking movement. I could see at once that something was wrong with him. His head was far too big. The veins in it stuck out too much, and looked too blue. But beside each lovely little ear was a curl of hair, perfect and silky and fine. I put out
25 my hand to touch.

Wordpool

miserable (line 3)
tenderness (8)
shells (15)
petals (15)
darling (19)

'Can I, Mum?' I said.

'Yes, of course.' She was smiling, but in that way that meant she was nearly crying too. She left me alone with Ben.

30 I may only have been twelve, and short-sighted, and spotty, but I knew how to fall in love. I fell in love with Ben at that moment.

'I don't care how disabled you are,' I whispered to him. 'I love you. I'll always love you. I'll protect you and look after you. If anyone's going to be mean to you, they'll have to deal 35 with me first.'

I bent over the cot, and kissed him. It was like kissing a rose. He moved a bit, and I felt he'd heard. It was silly, of course. He couldn't possibly understand, or know who I was, or even feel much at his age. He didn't even have his eyes open. 40 But I felt as if he loved me, too.

ELIZABETH LAIRD

Comprehension

1 What fears does Anna have at first?

2 What makes Anna's fears disappear?

3 How does Anna feel when her mother shows her Ben's toes?

4 What does Anna see and feel when she sees Ben's head?

5 What do you think Anna means when she says she 'fell in love' with Ben?

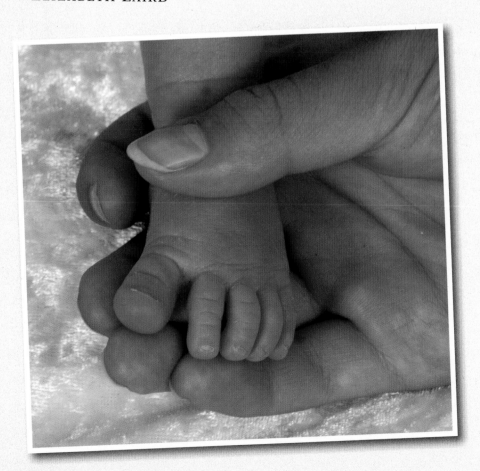

Looking closely

1 How does Anna describe her relief in the second paragraph? Why is it an appropriate description?

2 In the fourth paragraph there are two similes. Write them down and explain how they add to your understanding of what is happening in the story.

3 In the fifth paragraph the writer uses three adjectives one after the other to describe Ben's hair. Write them down and explain how they add to the description of baby Ben and how Anna feels about him.

4 In the final paragraph the writer uses a simile. Explain what it tells you about how Anna is feeling.

5 How many times does the writer use the words 'love', 'loved', or 'loving' in the story? What does this tell you about Anna and her family?

Talking points

1 What difference will Ben make to Anna and her family?

2 What difference will having Anna for a sister make to Ben's life?

Writing a letter

Imagine that you are Anna. Your favourite aunt has not seen Ben and wants to know all about him.

- Write a letter to your aunt telling her about Ben coming home and how you feel.
- Set out your letter with your address at the top.
  Start out by writing 'Dear Aunt Alice'.
- In the first paragraph, tell your aunt about what happened.
  In the second paragraph, tell her how you felt.

How can we best work together?

The cartoon pictures below have something to teach about communities. Look at the pictures of the donkeys with a partner. You can see that they are tied together. What happens?

Talking points

1 What are the donkeys doing in each picture?

2 What problem do the donkeys have?

3 How do they solve it?

4 What do you think these donkeys can teach us about solving a problem in our community?

5 What do you as a group think is the best way of resolving a difficult situation in a community?

163